An Analysis of

Edmund Gettier's

Is Justified True Belief Knowledge?

Jason Schukraft

Routledge
Taylor & Francis Group

LONDON AND NEW YORK

Published by Macat International Ltd
24:13 Coda Centre, 189 Munster Road, London SW6 6AW.

Distributed exclusively by Routledge
2 Park Square, Milton Park, Abingdon, Oxon OX14 4RN
605 Third Avenue, New York, NY 10017

Routledge is an imprint of the Taylor & Francis Group, an informa business

Copyright © 2017 by Macat International Ltd
Macat International has asserted its right under the Copyright, Designs and Patents Act
1988 to be identified as the copyright holder of this work.

www.macat.com
info@macat.com

Cataloguing in Publication Data
A catalogue record for this book is available from the British Library.
Library of Congress Cataloguing-in-Publication Data is available upon request.
Cover illustration: Etienne Gilfillan

ISBN 978-1-912302-98-7 (hardback)
ISBN 978-1-912127-49-8 (paperback)
ISBN 978-1-912281-86-2 (e-book)

Notice

CONTENTS

THE MACAT LIBRARY

The Macat Library is a series of unique academic explorations of seminal works in the humanities and social sciences – books and papers that have had a significant and widely recognised impact on their disciplines. It has been created to serve as much more than just a summary of what lies between the covers of a great book. It illuminates and explores the influences on, ideas of, and impact of that book. Our goal is to offer a learning resource that encourages critical thinking and fosters a better, deeper understanding of important ideas.

Each publication is divided into three Sections: Influences, Ideas, and Impact. Each Section has four Modules. These explore every important facet of the work, and the responses to it.

This Section-Module structure makes a Macat Library book easy to use, but it has another important feature. Because each Macat book is written to the same format, it is possible (and encouraged!) to cross-reference multiple Macat books along the same lines of inquiry or research. This allows the reader to open up interesting interdisciplinary pathways.

To further aid your reading, lists of glossary terms and people mentioned are included at the end of this book (these are indicated by an asterisk [*] throughout) – as well as a list of works cited.

Macat has worked with the University of Cambridge to identify the elements of critical thinking and understand the ways in which six different skills combine to enable effective thinking.
Three allow us to fully understand a problem; three more give us the tools to solve it. Together, these six skills make up the **PACIER** model of critical thinking. They are:

ANALYSIS – understanding how an argument is built
EVALUATION – exploring the strengths and weaknesses of an argument
INTERPRETATION – understanding issues of meaning

CREATIVE THINKING – coming up with new ideas and fresh connections
PROBLEM-SOLVING – producing strong solutions
REASONING – creating strong arguments

To find out more, visit **WWW.MACAT.COM.**

CRITICAL THINKING AND "IS JUSTIFIED TRUE BELIEF KNOWLEDGE?"

Primary critical thinking skill: ANALYSIS
Secondary critical thinking skill: REASONING

For 2,000 years, the standard philosophical model of knowledge was that it could be defined as a justified true belief. According to this way of thinking, we can know, for example, that we are human because [1] we believe ourselves to be human; [2] that belief is justified (others treat us as humans, not as dogs); and [3] the belief is true. This definition, which dates to Plato, was challenged by Edmund Gettier in one of the most influential works of philosophy published in the last century – a three page paper that produced two clear examples of justified true beliefs that could not, in fact, be considered knowledge.

Gettier's achievement rests on solid foundations provided by his mastery of the critical thinking skill of analysis. By understanding the way in which Plato – and every other epistemologist – had built their arguments, he was able to identify the relationships between the parts, and the assumptions that underpinned then. That precise understanding was what Gettier required to mount a convincing challenge to the theory – one that was bolstered by a reasoning skill that put his counter case pithily, and in a form his colleagues found all but unchallengeable.

ABOUT THE AUTHOR OF THE ORIGINAL WORK

Edmund Gettier was born in Baltimore in the United States in 1927. After finishing his studies, he began teaching at Wayne State University, in Detroit, Michigan. He needed to publish something to be considered for tenure (a permanent faculty position). So he wrote a short article and half-heartedly tried to have it published. When a leading philosophy journal actually did publish the piece, Gettier was quickly hailed because of the stunning originality of his thinking. Gettier went on to have a long teaching career, but seemed to remain unimpressed by the debates and continuing research his paper inspired.

ABOUT THE AUTHOR OF THE ANALYSIS

Jason Schukraft teaches philosophy at the University of Texas, Austin. His researches focus on philosophical intuition, epistemology, and the philosophy of the arts.

ABOUT MACAT

GREAT WORKS FOR CRITICAL THINKING

Macat is focused on making the ideas of the world's great thinkers accessible and comprehensible to everybody, everywhere, in ways that promote the development of enhanced critical thinking skills.

It works with leading academics from the world's top universities to produce new analyses that focus on the ideas and the impact of the most influential works ever written across a wide variety of academic disciplines. Each of the works that sit at the heart of its growing library is an enduring example of great thinking. But by setting them in context – and looking at the influences that shaped their authors, as well as the responses they provoked – Macat encourages readers to look at these classics and game-changers with fresh eyes. Readers learn to think, engage and challenge their ideas, rather than simply accepting them.

'Macat offers an amazing first-of-its-kind tool for interdisciplinary learning and research. Its focus on works that transformed their disciplines and its rigorous approach, drawing on the world's leading experts and educational institutions, opens up a world-class education to anyone.'

Andreas Schleicher
Director for Education and Skills, Organisation for Economic Co-operation and Development

'Macat is taking on some of the major challenges in university education ... They have drawn together a strong team of active academics who are producing teaching materials that are novel in the breadth of their approach.'

Prof Lord Broers,
former Vice-Chancellor of the University of Cambridge

'The Macat vision is exceptionally exciting. It focuses upon new modes of learning which analyse and explain seminal texts which have profoundly influenced world thinking and so social and economic development. It promotes the kind of critical thinking which is essential for any society and economy.
This is the learning of the future.'

Rt Hon Charles Clarke, former UK Secretary of State for Education

'The Macat analyses provide immediate access to the critical conversation surrounding the books that have shaped their respective discipline, which will make them an invaluable resource to all of those, students and teachers, working in the field.'

Professor William Tronzo, University of California at San Diego

WAYS IN TO THE TEXT

KEY POINTS

- Edmund Gettier is an important mid-twentieth-century American philosopher.

- "Is Justified True Belief Knowledge?" presented a counter-example to a longstanding philosophical theory of knowledge.

- The article, a mere 930 words long, transformed the philosophical study of knowledge and changed the research agenda of philosophers for decades. Gettier's work is philosophy at its most concise and its most powerful.

Who Is Edmund Gettier?

Edmund Gettier is an American philosopher who became famous for the one short article he published during his professional life, "Is Justified True Belief Knowledge?" He was born in Baltimore, Maryland in 1927 and studied philosophy, earning his PhD from Cornell University—an elite institution situated in Ithaca, New York—in 1961. By then Gettier was already a member of the faculty of Wayne State University in Detroit, Michigan. After getting his PhD, Gettier applied for tenure—that is, permanent academic job status. To get tenure, academics have to publish in peer-reviewed journals, but Gettier had not yet published anything. So, urged on by colleagues, he quickly wrote a short three-page article. The subject of the piece was the "justified true belief"* explanation of knowledge. This explanation—that a true belief is justified if it is well supported by the available evidence and that this constitutes knowledge—had been widely accepted for over two thousand years, at least since the ancient Greek philosopher Plato discussed it in the fourth century B.C.E. but Gettier set out to reject this explanation. He was persuaded to send his article to a leading philosophy journal, *Analysis*, which in turn published it in 1963. The article—only 930 words long—soon sparked a storm within the philosophy community, where most people believed that, incredibly, Gettier had succeeded in disproving the two-thousand-year-old standard model of knowledge.

Although his article made him famous among philosophers, Gettier has shown almost no interest in the decades' worth of debates it set off. That one three-page article was enough to win him tenure, and he went on to have a long career as a university philosophy teacher, moving to the University of Massachusetts in 1967 and it was the only scholarly article he ever published. In 2013, the University of Edinburgh in Scotland hosted an international conference to mark the 50-year anniversary of Gettier's famous article. Many of the world's leading epistemologists*—that is, philosophers who specialize in the nature of knowledge—attended the conference. True to form, Gettier declined to go.

What Does "Is Justified True Belief Knowledge?" Say?

Justified true belief—or JTB, as it is known—is how philosophers have traditionally understood what *knowledge* is. This has been the case since as long ago as the fourth century B.C.E., when Greek philosopher Plato discussed the subject. According to this way of thinking, I *know* that, for example, I am human, because: (1)

I believe I am human; (2) my belief is justified (people treat me like a human, not like a dog); and (3) it is true. In his 1963 paper, Gettier presented two cases in which a person has a justified true belief that is, nonetheless, *not* knowledge. Today, a large majority of philosophers accept Gettier's counter-examples as proof that JTB is not an adequate analysis of knowledge.

In one of Gettier's two examples, Smith and Jones have both applied for the same job. Smith believes on strong evidence that Jones will get the job (the company president told him). Smith also believes on strong evidence that Jones has 10 coins in his pocket (Smith has counted them). So Smith believes the man who will get the job has 10 coins in his pocket, which we can call proposition (P). In the end, however, it is Smith and not Jones who will get the job. But, unknown to Smith, he also happens to have 10 coins in his own pocket. So his belief turns out to be true. But it is true purely by accident, and therefore, says Gettier, it is not a case of knowledge; Smith does not *know* proposition (P).

Gettier's short article shook the philosophy world. For the first time in more than 2000 years, someone found a major flaw that seemed to disprove a bedrock theory of epistemology, the branch of philosophy that looks at the nature of knowledge. What's more, Gettier's article was brief and concise, presenting its arguments in a simple, straightforward way.

The article set off a flurry of activity in the philosophy community, activity that has continued, at least in some form, up to today. Inspired by Gettier's work, dozens of other scholars have come up with alternative counter-examples—cases in which JTB does not equal knowledge. Other scholars debated whether Gettier's arguments are correct. Some claimed his conclusion that the persons in his two cases did not *know* the proposition in question had not been proven, or that the intuition* Gettier used to form his conclusion was not universal—it would not be shared by people from other cultures. Today, a large majority of scholars side with Gettier in believing that justified true belief is not an adequate model of knowledge. Moreover, in recent years, a number of scholars have gone a step further, arguing that knowledge is a basic, primitive concept that cannot be fully analyzed.

Why Does "Is Justified True Belief Knowledge?" Matter?

With its focus on what it really means to know something, Gettier's article has influenced thinking in nearly all branches of philosophy. The article has been cited over 2,300 times since it first appeared. At a brief 930 words, it holds the highest citation-per-word ratio of any philosophical work ever published.[1]

The work also helped spark new ideas in other areas, including the philosophy of law.* Scholars in this field are interested in such questions as what makes a law court's decision correct, successful or moral. American legal scholar Michael Pardo* thinks that Gettier's work can help in answering these questions. Pardo argues for "a deeper connection between knowledge and legal proof" than legal scholars usually see as necessary.

Inspired by Gettier's counter-examples, Pardo presented a case he calls "Framed Defendant." In it, the police stop a driver, plant illegal drugs in his car, and arrest him for illegal possession. At his trial, he is found guilty on the basis of the testimony of the officers and the drugs they planted. However, it turns out the man was in fact carrying illegal drugs that were never discovered. So the verdict was true and justified (justified because the evidence presented at his trial was enough to convict him), but the truth of the verdict (that the man was carrying illegal drugs) is purely accidental.[2] The truth and the justifying evidence are disconnected. Pardo claims the court's verdict in this case was not "successful." He says sometimes knowledge—and not merely justified true belief—is required for a correct verdict.

The story of Gettier and his short article "Is Justified True Belief Knowledge?" provides a rare and inspiring example from the world of academia. It shows that, with a fresh insight that challenges a long-held idea, even an unknown junior scholar from an average university can have a huge impact on their academic field and beyond.

NOTES

1   John Turri, "In Gettier's Wake," in Stephen Hetherington, ed. Epistemology: The Key Thinkers (London: Continuum International Publishing Group, 2012).

2   Pardo, "The Gettier Problem and Legal Proof," Legal Theory 16, no. 1 (2010): 50.

SECTION 1
INFLUENCES

MODULE 1
THE AUTHOR AND THE
HISTORICAL CONTEXT

KEY POINTS

- "Is Justified True Belief Knowledge?" overturned an understanding that had held for over 2,000 years and, in doing so, revolutionized the philosophical study of knowledge.

- Gettier was educated by the leading philosophers of his day at Cornell University. At the time he wrote his article, conceptual analysis* was a popular method of philosophical investigation.

- Gettier's two famous counter-examples showed it was possible to have a belief that is both justified and true, but that is only true by chance. And so he argued that it is not "knowledge."

Why Read This Text?

Edmund Gettier wrote his pioneering article "Is Justified True Belief Knowledge?" in 1963. It is a rare work of philosophy because it is so brief, so clear and so original. Herman Cappelen,* a leading philosopher at the University of St. Andrews, calls the success of Gettier's three-page paper "extremely unusual in philosophy."[1] In the paper, Gettier challenges a long-standing philosophical idea, known as the "justified true belief" analysis of knowledge* (often abbreviated to JTB). For example, according to the JTB analysis, to know that Cairo is the capital of Egypt, three conditions must hold: one must *believe* that Cairo is the capital of Egypt, this belief must be *justified* by evidence, and it must be *true* that Cairo is the capital of Egypt.

66 There was a time when for just about everyone,
knowledge was the same as justified true belief. That
view was done away with by Edmund Gettier. 99

Angelika Kratzer "Facts: Particulars or Information Units?

In the essay, Gettier shows it is possible to form a justified true belief merely by chance. He argues that beliefs founded on luck are not knowledge. At the time he wrote the essay, Gettier was a young and unknown philosopher, yet he forced other philosophers to rethink the JTB model of knowledge, a theory that had stood for more than 2,000 years. This shows the remarkable power of Gettier's thinking.

"Is Justified True Belief Knowledge?" revolutionized the discipline of epistemology,* the philosophical examination of knowledge. Gettier's accomplishment had an impact throughout the philosophy community and its various specialist areas. It influenced debates in the philosophy of language,* the philosophy of law,* metaphysics* (the branch of philosophy that looks at the nature of reality), and philosophical methodology.*[2] Gettier's two famous examples that overturned the justified true belief formula have come to be seen as the most famous counter-examples in twentieth-century philosophy. The degree of philosophical change his two cases sparked rarely occurs in such a short period.

Most impressively, Gettier provoked this change using just 930 words. Having been routinely cited for 50 years, Gettier's essay now holds the highest citation-per-word ratio of any philosophical work ever published.[3]

Author's Life

Edmund Gettier was born in Baltimore, Maryland in 1927 and grew up to study philosophy, publishing his seminal paper "Is

Justified True Belief Knowledge" in 1963. He had four main intellectual influences:

- The philosophical climate of the period
- His mentors at Cornell University, where he received his PhD in 1961
- His colleagues at Wayne State University, where he was affiliated
- The areas he chose to research before publishing.

At Cornell, Gettier was mentored by Norman Malcolm* and Max Black,* two leading philosophers of language.* Both men were themselves heavily influenced by the Austrian-British philosopher Ludwig Wittgenstein.* This in turn contributed to Gettier's interest in Wittgenstein's writings on mathematics, logic, and the philosophy of logic. The leading British philosopher Bertrand Russell* was an early champion of analytic approaches to philosophical problems and had a big impact on Wittgenstein. Interestingly, although Gettier's counter-examples to the justified true belief account of knowledge are original, Russell made similar arguments himself.[4] Russell, too, was interested in the nature of knowledge and, like Gettier, he used an example involving an individual coming to a true belief by accident to illustrate a point about knowledge. However, this example is different from Gettier's examples because, unlike Gettier, who is explicit that his subject's true belief is justified, Russell did not discuss the issue of whether his individual has a *justified* true belief.

Gettier was educated during the heyday of conceptual analysis* in Anglo-American philosophy. Conceptual analysis involves taking a concept, such as knowledge, and searching for the set of necessary and sufficient conditions* for that concept to be demonstrated. For example, the analysis of the concept "bachelor" might give "adult unmarried male" as the necessary and sufficient conditions. Gettier was working at Wayne State University in Detroit, which was a hub of this sort of philosophical activity. It was here that he met Keith Lehrer* and Alvin Plantinga,* who would go on to have prominent careers in epistemology. At first Gettier didn't want to publish his findings, considering them to be only minor contributions to the theory of knowledge. It was only after he was pushed to do so by his colleagues that Gettier changed his mind.[5]

Author's Background

Edmund Gettier's short essay challenges the traditional view that knowledge consists of justified true beliefs. The paper consists of two counter-examples to this traditional view. In one, a job applicant ("Smith") comes to believe, truly and justifiably, that the person who will get the job has 10 coins in his pocket. Smith forms this judgment on the basis of his mistaken belief that an acquaintance ("Jones") will get the job, and the true belief that Jones has 10 coins in his pocket. In fact, Smith himself gets the job—and, by pure coincidence, Smith himself has 10 coins in his pocket. In short, Smith has come to the right belief, but only by chance. Gettier declares this to be a case of justified true belief, but not of knowledge.

At the time Gettier wrote his piece, the justified true belief account of knowledge—the view that a belief rises to the level of knowledge when it is both well supported by the available evidence and true—was widespread among philosophers. Indeed, this account of knowledge dates back to two dialogues of the ancient Greek philosopher Plato*—the *Theaetetus* and the *Meno*—from the fourth century B.C.E. Gettier's paper caused most philosophers to abandon this traditional understanding of knowledge for the first time in more than two thousand years.

NOTES

1   Herman Cappenden, *Philosophy Without Intuitions* (Oxford: Oxford University Press, 2012), 194, fn. 9.

2   See, for example, Max Deutsch, "Intuitions, Counter-Examples, and Experimental Philosophy," *Review of Philosophy and Psychology* 1, no. 3 (2010): 447–60; Cappelen, *Philosophy Without Intuitions*; George Bealer, "On the Possibility of Philosophical Knowledge," *Philosophical Perspectives* 10 (1996): 1–34; Michael Pardo, "The Gettier Problem and Legal Proof," *Legal Theory* 16, no. 1 (2010): 37–57.

3   John Turri, "In Gettier's Wake," in Stephen Hetherington, ed. *Epistemology: The Key Thinkers* (London: Continuum International Publishing Group, 2012).

4   See chapter 13 of Bertrand Russell, *The Problems of Philosophy* (Oxford: Oxford University Press, 1912/1959).

5   Louis P. Pojman, *The Theory of Knowledge: Classical and Contemporary Readings* (Belmont, CA: Wadsworth Publishing Company, 1999), 138.

MODULE 2
ACADEMIC CONTEXT

KEY POINTS

- Gettier made a big impact on the field of epistemology* — the study of the nature of knowledge. Epistemologists have long been interested in the necessary and sufficient conditions* required for a fact to be known.

- Since Plato* more than 2,000 years ago, philosophers have recognized the importance of *justification* to knowledge. Knowledge was defined as true belief that is backed up by evidence—until Gettier showed that this definition is not adequate.

- Gettier used the "conceptual analysis" approach, which was popular at the time. His powerful counter-examples challenged the justified true belief analysis of knowledge.

The Work in its Context

Edmund Gettier's 1963 paper "Is Justified True Belief Knowledge?" makes important contributions to the field of epistemology, which is normally taken to be one of the three main branches of philosophy, alongside metaphysics* and ethics.* Epistemologists are interested in questions such as "What is knowledge?" and "Why is knowledge better than mere true belief?"

Research in the field of epistemology impacts thinking outside philosophy. The question of knowledge, for example, often influences our judgments of moral responsibility or guilt. If a friend demands to know why you have not given her a birthday present, answering that you did not know it was her birthday is a way of excusing yourself of guilt or blame. If the conditions under which

> **❝ Before 1963, the concept of knowledge was either left unanalyzed or defined more or less as true justified belief. ❞**
> Louis P. Pojman, *The Theory of Knowledge: Classical and Contemporary Readings*

facts such as birthdays can be known are unclear, then issues of responsibility or blame will be hard to decide. Epistemologists seek to understand those conditions.

One of the traditional goals of epistemology is to discover the necessary and sufficient conditions for knowledge. A necessary condition is a condition that must be met in order for some further state to exist. For instance, being unmarried is a necessary condition for being a bachelor but it is not sufficient, because unmarried women are not bachelors (they are called bachelorettes or spinsters). A sufficient condition is one that guarantees that some further state exists: being from Cairo, for instance, is a sufficient condition for being Egyptian, but it is not necessary since those from Alexandria are also Egyptian.

Overview of the Field

The ancient Greek philosopher Plato was perhaps the first to offer something like necessary and sufficient conditions for knowledge. In particular, he was the first to clearly show the importance of *justification* to knowledge. Belief is justified when it is well supported by evidence. If that belief is also true, then, according to Plato, that amounts to knowledge. Plato addresses this issue in two fourth-century B.C.E. dialogues, the *Theaetetus* and the *Meno*.

In the *Theaetetus*, Plato writes that it is "true judgment with an account that is knowledge; true judgment without an account falls outside of knowledge."[1] Here "account" (*logos*, in the Greek) means something like explanation or justification. In the *Meno*, Plato writes: "When true beliefs are anchored, they become pieces of knowledge and they become stable. That's why knowledge is more valuable than true belief, and the difference between the two is that knowledge has been anchored."[2] Again, "anchored" means something very much like justified.

For more than 2,000 years, philosophers pointed to Plato's insight to distinguish mere true belief from genuine knowledge. For knowledge to be genuine, a person's true belief must be justified. It was widely thought that this was the last major breakthrough needed to understand the nature of knowledge. Essentially, Plato had it right, and although there were minor details to work out, the broad epistemological framework—knowledge as justified true belief—was widely accepted.

Academic Influences

Gettier's essay appeared during a period that has been called the "sunset years of conceptual analysis."*[3] In philosophy, conceptual analysis means taking some concept of interest—knowledge, for example—and searching for the set of necessary and sufficient conditions under which that concept holds true.

The practice of conceptual analysis traces its roots back to Plato's dialogues, in which his characters would seek the definition of some concept, such as piety—being religious or virtuous—(in the *Euthyphro*) or justice (in the *Republic*).

Among philosophers, the popularity of conceptual analysis has gone up and down over the years, but by the middle part of the twentieth century, it was at its peak. In particular, epistemologists thought the necessary and sufficient conditions for knowledge—namely, justification, truth, and belief—had been proven.

Gettier's paper can be seen as being situated in this intellectual environment. The justified true belief account of knowledge is a leading example of the thinking behind conceptual analysis. Although Gettier showed that the idea was not adequate, it is clear that he was nevertheless working within the framework of the conceptual analysis school of thought.

The essay was celebrated for its original and brilliant counter-examples. Within conceptual analysis, coming up with counter-examples to disprove an established idea is highly valued. The mere *possibility* that a person could have a justified true belief *without* having knowledge is enough to disprove the whole justified true belief analysis of knowledge.

Shortly after Gettier's article appeared, the popularity of conceptual analysis in philosophical circles began to decline, largely due to the work of another American philosopher, Willard Van Orman Quine,* and his followers. Because of this, one could imagine that if Gettier's paper had appeared a decade later than it did, its influence would have been far less widespread than it actually was.

NOTES

1   Plato, *Complete Works*, ed. John M. Cooper (Indianapolis: Hackett Publishing Company, 1997), 201d.

2   Plato, *Meno and Other Dialogues*, trans. Robin Waterfield (Oxford: Oxford University Press, 2005), 98a.

3   William Lycan, "On the Gettier Problem," in Stephen Hetherington, ed. *Epistemology Futures* (Oxford: Clarendon Press, 2006): 150–1.

MODULE 3
THE PROBLEM

KEY POINTS

- Epistemologists* had thought for a long time that knowledge should be understood as beliefs that are both true and justified. Gettier's counter-examples changed traditional thinking on this subject.

- At the time Gettier's paper was published, philosophers thought their standard model might be refined a little, but certainly not disproven. Even Gettier himself did not at first realize that his paper was going to overthrow the accepted theory.

- When Gettier's work appeared, many philosophers started looking for a "fourth condition" for knowledge to add to justification, truth, and belief in order to save the traditional model. But as soon as one was proposed, it was immediately opposed.

Core Question

Edmund Gettier's short article "Is Justified True Belief Knowledge?" clearly has just one core question—the one it asks in the title. Gettier addresses this core question by offering two counter-examples to the view that knowledge is indeed identical to justified true belief.* The paper's key idea is that it is entirely possible that justified true belief *can* fail to be knowledge.

Historically, the most popular answer to the question "What is knowledge?" was: "Justified true beliefs." According to this analysis of knowledge, in order for an individual to know some proposition* (meaning a fact or an idea), that individual must believe the proposition, the proposition must be true, and the individual's belief

> **❝** The Gettier result that justified true belief was insufficient for knowledge did come as a surprise, and resonated with an audience of philosophers who had largely been committed to one or another form of JTB theory.**❞**
>
> Jennifer Nagel, "Intuitions and Experiments"

in the proposition must be justified. In order for some person—Ahmed, say—to know that Cairo is the capital of Egypt, Ahmed must believe that Cairo is the capital of Egypt, Cairo must in fact be the capital of Egypt, and Ahmed must base his belief on reasonable and reliable evidence, such as an up-to-date map. Justification, belief, and truth are individually necessary and jointly sufficient* for knowledge, according to this school of thought. Gettier's paper challenges this analysis of knowledge.

Gettier's central question is the title of the paper: *Is justified true belief knowledge?* His answer is that it is not. He supports his answer with two counter-examples in which he presents an individual whom he declares to have a justified true belief, but who still does not have knowledge. These two counter-examples would prove to be enormously influential, and together they shook up the whole field of epistemology.

The Participants

Roderick Chisholm,* a prominent philosopher working at Brown University in the United States, best expresses the dominant ideology or theory of the time. Chisholm wanted to find the necessary and sufficient conditions* for knowledge, and his results, published in 1957, were squarely in line with the tradition dating back to Plato. Chisholm claims that an individual S knows a proposition P if and only if:

1. S accepts P,
2. S has adequate evidence for P, and
3. P is true.[1]

Notice that condition 1 is about the same as S *believing* P, and condition 2 is about the same as S's belief in P being *justified*.

Chisholm is a good representative of the type of epistemologist targeted by Gettier's paper.[2] In many ways, Chisholm represents the philosophical orthodoxy of the time. The expectation among epistemologists working in the 1950s was that this tradition would be refined and the details worked out more precisely, but no major changes were expected. This expectation colors Gettier's paper. The tone of the essay is one of revision (updating), not revolution (that is, disproving the accepted formula). Nowhere does Gettier argue that his cases will force philosophers to give up the old framework. In fact, there is evidence that he considered his work a minor contribution to the theory of knowledge.[3] Yet Gettier's results exposed a much deeper problem in the justified true belief model than even he realized.

The Contemporary Debate

The impact of Gettier's counter-examples was immediate and widespread. Most philosophers agreed that the justified true belief theory could no longer be accepted in its current form. Yet many were reluctant to give up the traditional approach entirely. One remarked that "the widespread reaction was that [the 'justified true belief' model] was pretty close to the truth, and it just needed some patching up."[4] These philosophers admitted that, yes, Gettier had successfully overthrown the most naïve and simplistic version of the model. Surely, they went on, the theory could be repaired to avoid Gettier-style counter-examples? A cottage industry sprang up seeking to find the so-called fourth condition for knowledge to add to justification, truth, and belief.

Philosophers differed on the exact nature of this fourth condition. But gradually almost all agreed that knowledge could not be the result of luck. Gettier, however, had shown that it was possible to form a justified true belief by chance. If the fourth condition could rule out *accidental* justified true belief, then the spirit of the theory could be saved. But as philosophers proposed different ideas for the fourth condition, other philosophers rushed to offer counter-examples that disproved them. These counter-examples were based on Gettier's original cases, and were designed to show that these attempts could not save the theory.[5]

This back-and-forth, with new proposals to explain what knowledge is, followed by counter-examples claiming to disprove those proposals, made up the major battlefield in epistemology during the period, roughly, of the 1960 and 1970s.

NOTES

1   Roderick M. Chisholm, *Perceiving: a Philosophical Study* (Ithaca, NY: Cornell University Press, 1957), 16. Quoted in Edmund L. Gettier, "Is Justified True Belief Knowledge?" *Analysis* 23, no. 6 (1963): 121.

2   See also A. J. Ayer, *The Problem of Knowledge* (London: Macmillan, 1956).

3   Louis P. Pojman, *The Theory of Knowledge: Classical and Contemporary Readings* (Belmont, CA: Wadsworth Publishing Company, 1999), 138.

4   Steven Hales, "The Faculty of Intuition," *Analytic Philosophy,* 53 no. 2 (2012): 187.

5   See, for example, Michael Clark, "Knowledge and Grounds: A Comment on Mr. Gettier's Paper," *Analysis* 24, no. 2 (1963): 46–8 and Alvin Goldman, "Discrimination and Perceptual Knowledge," *Journal of Philosophy* 73, (1976): 771–91.

MODULE 4
THE AUTHOR'S CONTRIBUTION

KEY POINTS

- Gettier's aim was purely negative. He wanted to prove that the justified true belief (JTB) theory was wrong.

- Gettier's paper showed the power of counter-examples in philosophy. One would have been enough to demolish the JTB model. He provided two.

- While Gettier's counter-examples were startlingly original, his methods were not. Philosophers have used counter-examples as a form of argument since at least the time of Plato in the fourth century B.C.E.

Author's Aims

Edmund Gettier's groundbreaking article "Is Justified True Belief Knowledge?" attacks the long-held justified true belief model of knowledge.* According to this theory, a person knows a proposition*—a fact or idea—when (and only when) he or she believes it, that belief is true, and that belief is well supported by the available evidence.

The main—indeed, the only—theme of Gettier's short paper is that justified true belief alone is not enough for knowledge. He claims it is possible for an individual to have a justified true belief that "P is so" without having *knowledge* that "P is so." Hence, sometimes a belief that is both true and well supported by the available evidence nevertheless is not enough to be called knowledge. What was so remarkable about Gettier's work is that he was able to prove this possibility with two simple examples.

Gettier wants to show that it is possible for an individual to have a justified true belief without having knowledge. In this sense, his

❝ Gettier famously showed that there are easily constructed examples that satisfy the traditional definition of knowledge ... but that nonetheless do not seem intuitively to be cases of knowledge.❞

Laurence BonJour, "The Myth of Knowledge"

aim is purely negative. He wants to overturn a leading philosophical theory, but he does not offer a theory to replace it. His aim is stated in a clear plan, and he does not depart from this aim in any important way. The short paper, a mere 930 words in length, is a very efficient piece of philosophy.

Approach

Gettier outlines his target in the paper's opening paragraph: "Various attempts have been made in recent years to state necessary and sufficient conditions* for someone's knowing a given proposition. The attempts have often been such that they can be stated in a form similar to the following:

S knows that P IFF [i.e. if and only if]
(i) P is true,
(ii) S believes that P, and
(iii) S is justified in believing that P."[1]

Gettier next lays out his plan of attack. He writes, "I shall argue that (a) is false in that the conditions stated therein do not constitute a *sufficient* condition for the truth of the proposition that S knows that P."[2] He executes this plan by presenting two original counter-examples to the justified true belief analysis of knowledge.

Gettier's paper is a lesson in the power of counter-examples in philosophy. Gettier's opponents believed that in all cases justified true belief was also knowledge. Therefore, it would take just one counter-example—that is, one instance of justified true belief without knowledge—to falsify this position. For good measure, Gettier gives us two. Using these two cases in a creative and brilliantly argued way, Gettier is able to overthrow a philosophical theory that had stood for millennia with a paper a mere three pages long.

Contribution in Context

"Is Justified True Belief Knowledge?" was Gettier's first—and only—published paper. So the origins of his famous counter-examples cannot be traced to any earlier works. The counter-examples seem to be original, but how they were thought up is unknown. A similar example appears in a 1912 work by the British philosopher Bertrand Russell,* but there is little reason to believe that Gettier took his cases from Russell.[3]

While Gettier's ideas were novel, his methods were not. Rejecting an idea by use of counter-example is as old as philosophy itself, dating back at least to the fourth-century B.C.E. Greek philosopher Plato.*[4] In Plato's dialogues, one person will propose a universal definition of some philosophical concept (justice, piety [being religious or virtuous], or temperance [abstaining from alcohol], for example), while the other characters will attempt to find instances of the concept not being captured by the proposed definition. If a counter-example is found, the first character will propose an updated definition, and the search for counter-examples will begin anew. This back-and-forth process continues until a good definition is discovered.

Gettier's counter-examples represent one part of the broader epistemological* discussion of the 1960s and 1970s. What makes Gettier's essay one of the most influential papers in twentieth-century analytic philosophy is how well his counter-examples (and the dozens of similar counter-examples they inspired) could stand up to any attempts to update the definition of knowledge.

NOTES

1   Edmund L. Gettier, "Is Justified True Belief Knowledge?" *Analysis* 23, no. 6 (1963): 121.

2   Gettier, "Is Justified True Belief," 121.

3   Bertrand Russell, *The Problems of Philosophy* (Oxford: Oxford University Press, 1912/1959): 131.

4   See, for example, Plato's *Euthyphro* in *Complete Works*, ed. John M. Cooper (Indianapolis: Hackett Publishing Company, 1997).

SECTION 2
IDEAS

MODULE 5
MAIN IDEAS

KEY POINTS

- Before Gettier, the justified true belief (JTB) model of knowledge* was widely seen as a general analysis. All JTB was knowledge, and all knowledge was JTB.

- Gettier's famous counter-examples, however, tried to show that justified true beliefs formed merely by chance or accident are not knowledge.

- Yet Gettier's argument seems to rely on intuition* to a certain extent, and this side of his work has recently become controversial.

Key Themes

Edmund Gettier's paper "Is Justified True Belief Knowledge?" attacks the long-held justified true belief model of knowledge. In order to understand Gettier's challenge, one must first understand the model, and how philosophers were thinking about it in the 1960s, when Gettier wrote his paper.

The justified true belief model of knowledge was a theory in epistemology.* Epistemology is a branch of philosophy that investigates the nature of knowledge and related concepts, like justification and rationality. One method used in epistemology is conceptual analysis.* This is the process of breaking down a concept of interest (in this case knowledge) into simpler parts. Although its popularity has gone up and down over the years, conceptual analysis has often played a big role in philosophy. The seventeenth-century philosopher René Descartes* described the aim of conceptual analysis as follows: "If we perfectly understand a

> ❝ Gettier problems arise in the theory of knowledge when it is only by chance that a justified true belief is true. Since the belief might easily have been false in these cases, it is normally concluded that they are not instances of knowledge. ❞
>
> Linda Zagzebski, "The Inescapability of Gettier Problems"

problem we must abstract it from every superfluous [i.e. unneeded] conception, reduce it to its simplest terms and, by means of an enumeration [listing all the parts], divide it up into the smallest possible parts."[1] The justified true belief model of knowledge states that knowledge (as the name of the theory implies) is made up of justification, truth, and belief.

It is helpful to remember that the JTB theory of knowledge is meant to be a general model. According to this model, all cases of justified true belief are cases of knowledge, and each time you have knowledge, you have justified true belief. So Gettier only needed to find one counter-example to disprove the analysis. However, he challenges the model by offering not one but two cases in which an individual has a justified true belief but lacks knowledge.

Exploring the Ideas

Gettier offers two original examples to show that the accepted account of knowledge is not true.

In the more famous of his two cases, Gettier invites his reader to consider two job applicants, Smith and Jones.[2]

Suppose that Smith has good evidence for the following proposition,* which we will call (a):

> *(a) Jones is the man who will get the job, and Jones has 10 coins in his pocket.*

Smith has personally counted the coins in Jones's pocket, and he has been assured by the president of the company that Jones will be offered the job. In other words, he has good reason to believe the proposition.

If that proposition were true, then proposition (b) would also be true:

(b) The man who will get the job has 10 coins in his pocket.

Smith has good reason to believe that Jones is the man who will get the job, and that Jones has 10 coins in his pocket—proposition (a). Because he sees the relationship between the two propositions, Smith also has good reason to believe the second proposition (b).

Gettier's twist is that, although Smith doesn't know it, he also has 10 coins in his own pocket. Furthermore, in the end, Smith himself, and not Jones, is the one who gets the job.

The man who will get the job does indeed have 10 coins in his pocket. Proposition (b) is therefore true, but it's not true for the reason that Smith thinks it is true, after all, the first proposition (a) is false.

So, according to Gettier, Smith does not *know* proposition (b).

Recall, however, that proposition (b) is true; that Smith believes the proposition; and that Smith has good reason to believe that the proposition is true. In other words, Smith has a justified true belief in that proposition. Smith therefore satisfies the traditional requirements for knowledge of that proposition.

So if Gettier is right and Smith does not in fact have knowledge of proposition (b), then Gettier has found a counter-example to the justified true belief account of knowledge.

Language and Expression

Gettier's analysis of why his counter-examples succeed in disproving the justified true belief account is very limited. He does make some brief comments suggesting that an element of luck prevents the individuals in his cases from attaining knowledge. Mostly, he relies on his readers to come naturally to the same conclusions he does concerning the cases.

It is useful, then, not to think of Gettier's original cases as isolated counter-examples to the justified true belief model. Once an understanding of the basic structure of the so-called Gettier cases is reached, it is a simple matter to generate other counter-examples to the JTB model. By the mid-1980s, there were already more than 90 such examples in circulation.[3] For this reason, it is important not to get lost in the details of any particular Gettier-style thought experiment.* Instead, it is better to focus on what these sorts of cases reveal about the nature of knowledge.

The brief way in which Gettier draws conclusions from his cases has sometimes made it hard for readers to fully understand the examples. Gettier merely claims it is "clear that Smith does not know" the second proposition (b), and he expects his audience to form the same conclusion naturally.[4] When Gettier's article first appeared, most philosophers agreed with him and were forced to either give up or change the traditional account of knowledge that they had used.[5] Indeed, for over 50 years, since the publication of the paper in 1963, the vast majority of philosophers have been happy to go along with Gettier's conclusions. Recently, however, a growing number of philosophers have begun to question them. Some critics argue that his conclusions are not as convincing as they may have first appeared.[6] Other philosophers have gone so far as to challenge Gettier's methodology itself. They claim that rather than proving his conclusions with clear logic, Gettier's arguments appeal too much to mere intuition.[7]

NOTES

1   René Descartes, *Philosophical Writings of Descartes*, 3 vols., trans. John Cottingham, Robert Stoothoff, Dugald Murdoch, and Anthony Kenny (Cambridge: Cambridge University Press, 1984–91): vol. 1, 51.

2   Edmund L. Gettier, "Is Justified True Belief Knowledge?" *Analysis* 23, no. 6 (1963): 122.

3   For an overview, see Robert Shope, *The Analysis of Knowing: A Decade of Research* (Princeton, NJ: Princeton University Press, 1983).

4   Gettier, "Is Justified True Belief," 122.

5   See Shope, *Analysis of Knowing,* for an overview of reaction to Gettier's paper.

6   See Jonathan M. Weinberg, Shaun Nichols and Stephen Stich, "Normativity and Epistemic Intuitions," *Philosophical Topics* 29 (2001): 429–60.

7   See Brian Weatherson, "What Good Are Counterexamples?" *Philosophical Studies* 115 (2003): 1–31.

SECONDARY IDEAS

KEY POINTS

- Gettier's paper contains a second example that is also a case where someone has a correct answer, but they have reached it by accident, and therefore cannot be said to *know* the correct answer.

- The widespread view among philosophers was that Gettier's examples appealed to his readers' intuition,* as opposed to their reasoning.

- Today that view is challenged by scholars who think the importance of intuition in philosophy is overstated.

Other Ideas

Edmund Gettier's "Is Justified True Belief Knowledge?" challenges the justified true belief model of knowledge* with two decisive counter-examples.

In the less famous of his two cases, Gettier invites his reader to consider three individuals, Smith, Jones and Brown.[1]

Suppose Smith has good evidence for the following proposition,* which we call (a):

(a) Jones owns a Ford.

Smith's belief that Jones owns a Ford is well supported by the available evidence. Smith has known Jones for a long time, and during that time, Jones has always owned a car made by Ford. Moreover, Jones has just offered Smith a ride while driving a Ford. Smith's belief in proposition (a) is therefore justified.

❝ Suppose we philosophers know that a subject in a Gettier case does not know. How do we know this? The traditional answer is: By *thinking* about the case. **❞**
Max Deutsch, "Experimental Philosophy and the Theory of Reference"

Now consider the further proposition, which we will call (b):

(b) Either Jones owns a Ford, or Brown is in Barcelona.

Smith has no idea where Brown is, but he is confident that (b) is true.

Why? The proposition "Either Jones owns a Ford, or Brown is in Barcelona" is a disjunction*—that is, a sentence in which two or more parts (called the "disjuncts") are connected by "or." A disjunction is true if—and only if—one or more of the disjuncts is true (as opposed to an "exclusive disjunction," which is true when one of the disjuncts is true, but is false if both are true).

So if Jones in fact does own a Ford, then (b) is true. Smith's belief that Jones owns a Ford is justified, and he sees the relationship between (a) and (b), so Smith's belief in (b) is also justified. Keep in mind that Smith has no idea whatsoever where Brown is— Barcelona is just a randomly chosen location.

Here, however, is the twist.

Proposition (b) is in fact true—but not for the reason Smith thinks. It turns out that the car Jones was driving is a rental car; Jones does not own a car at all, let alone a Ford. By mere chance, and unknown to Smith, Brown really is in Barcelona.

To summarize: Smith believes (b), Smith's belief in (b) is justified, and (b) is true. Thus, all of the conditions of the traditional justified true belief model of knowledge are satisfied.

Nevertheless, according to Gettier, Smith does not have knowledge of proposition (b). If Gettier's judgment about this case is correct, then it follows that the justified true belief model of knowledge must be false.

Exploring the Ideas

With only 930 words, Gettier's paper has no room to explore any secondary ideas. The essay is wholly devoted to disproving the justified true belief model of knowledge. The article has, however, played an important secondary role in philosophical conversations outside epistemology,* the philosophical examination of knowledge. Because of its remarkable success, Gettier's essay is often studied by those interested in philosophical methodology,* where researchers seek to describe and analyze the *methods* philosophers use to construct and disprove philosophical theories.

Scholars in this field often assume that Gettier's counter-examples rely on intuitive judgment. According to this reading, Gettier does not argue that the individuals in his cases hold justified true beliefs, but lack knowledge; rather, he simply presents the cases, delivers his intuitive conclusion, and hopes his readers will agree. Some philosophers applaud this method; others attack it. Until very recently, however, few of them have questioned whether this is indeed the correct way to describe Gettier's approach.

Today, scholars such as Herman Cappelen* and Max Deutsch* are beginning to doubt this understanding of Gettier's methodology. Deutsch writes, "Intuitions play no evidential role in [Gettier's argument]."[2] These philosophers argue that reliance on intuition—as opposed to reasoning—is not as widespread in philosophy as is often assumed. They also argue that the traditional reading of Gettier's paper overlooks important aspects of his paper that are independent of intuition. Both writers would welcome a reinterpretation of the methodology behind Gettier's work.[3]

Overlooked

There is little agreement in philosophy about the nature of intuition and its value in proving or disproving theories. In order to find common ground in these debates, philosophers try to find examples of philosophical intuitions at work. Gettier's famous counter-examples are frequently cited as such examples.[4]

It is interesting to note that the word "intuition" does not appear in Gettier's text. This may, of course, tell us very little, since it is possible to appeal to intuition without mentioning it openly. Nevertheless, this simple fact is revealing.

In the first case, Gettier presents the conclusion—that Smith does not know that the man who will end up getting the job has 10 coins in his pocket. Then he immediately gives a reason to think Smith's belief (which happens to be correct) does not qualify as knowledge. He notes that the proposition that Smith believes in is "true in virtue of the number of coins in Smith's pocket, while Smith does not know how many coins are in Smith's pocket, and bases his belief [that the man who will get the job has 10 coins in his pocket] on a count of the coins in Jones's pocket, whom he falsely believes to be the man who will get the job."[5] Some authors take this sentence—which is frequently overlooked—to mean that Gettier did not intend intuition to play a role in his argument.[6]

A new interpretation of Gettier's text, weighted towards the author's reliance on philosophical reasoning rather than on intuition, may increase the power of his counter-examples. Those who do not share the intuitive judgment that Smith does not know, can be brought around by argument, rather than by mere encouragement to think harder about the case. This new focus would also change the role that Gettier's paper plays in debates about philosophical methodology.*

NOTES

1   Edmund L. Gettier, "Is Justified True Belief Knowledge?" *Analysis* 23, no. 6 (1963): 122.

2   Max Deutsch, "Intuitions, Counter-Examples, and Experimental Philosophy," *Review of Philosophy and Psychology* 1, no. 3 (2010): 453.

3   For an overview, see Herman Cappelen, *Philosophy without Intuitions* (Oxford: Oxford University Press, 2012).

4   See, for example, George Bealer, "On the Possibility of Philosophical Knowledge," *Philosophical Perspectives* 10 (1996): 1–34; Jonathan Weinberg, Shaun Nichols, and Stephen Stich, "Normativity and Epistemic Intuitions," *Philosophical Topics* 29 (2001): 429–60; Jennifer Nagel, "Intuitions and Experiments: A Defense of the Case Method in Epistemology," *Philosophy and Phenomenological Research* 85, no 3 (2012): 495–527.

5   Edmund L. Gettier, "Is Justified True Belief Knowledge?" *Analysis* 23, no. 6 (1963): 122.

6   See, for example, Deutsch, "Intuitions, Counter-Examples, and Experimental Philosophy."

MODULE 7
ACHIEVEMENT

KEY POINTS

- Gettier's brief paper has the highest citation-per-word ratio of any philosophical work ever published, and has had a big impact on philosophy.

- More recently, some scholars have argued that agreeing with Gettier's intuitive conclusion—that the persons in his examples don't *know* the fact they accidentally got right—depends on your cultural background.

- Gettier's work is not at all well known outside the field of philosophy, but it has nonetheless influenced other fields, including law.

Assessing the Argument

Edmund Gettier's short 1963 article "Is Justified True Belief Knowledge?" challenged the then-widespread philosophical belief that knowledge could be explained as justified true belief.* The goal of Gettier's paper was to overturn this long-standing position in epistemology.*

Gettier's success in reaching and influencing his target audience went beyond anything he could have imagined. The attention the paper received far outstripped what would be expected for a three-page article from a junior scholar at an uncelebrated university.

Gettier's essay has continued to be relevant over the last five decades thanks to a large number of philosophical examples based on his original cases that have been offered up by other scholars. Indeed, the term "Gettier case" has become a common philosophical term to refer to any thought experiment* which combines the following two features:

> **❝** If a certain intuitive response to some Gettier case works for the majority of epistemologists, we have no guarantee that it will work for others outside our professional club, and no good reason—the experimentalists argue—to suppose that it supplies genuine evidence about the nature of knowledge. **❞**
>
> Jennifer Nagel, "Intuitions and Experiments"

1. The main character of the story forms a true belief that is well supported by the available evidence.

2. Although the belief is justified, the truth of the belief is not confirmed by the available evidence, but, instead, is somehow due to chance.

Almost all epistemologists*—philosophers investigating the nature of knowledge—agree that the justified true beliefs in Gettier cases do not equal knowledge. Gettier was the first philosopher to recognize that such cases were possible. As such, nearly every important work in epistemology produced since 1963 owes a debt, either directly or indirectly, to Gettier's paper. The article has been cited over 2,300 times since it first appeared. At a brief 930 words, it now holds the highest citation-per-word ratio of any philosophical work ever published.[1]

Achievement in Context

Modern readers will appreciate Gettier's paper best if they share his intuitive judgments. Gettier concludes that the person in each of his two examples may believe a fact that turns out to be true by accident. But they don't *know* that fact. Most of Gettier's readers have been British or American, and recently some philosophers have begun to wonder if readers from different backgrounds might interpret the paper differently. Those asking this question belong to a branch of philosophy known as "experimental philosophy."* Many experimental philosophers argue that Gettier's conclusions—sometimes called "Gettier intuitions"*—are not so common outside the community of professional philosophers, and even outside western culture, and argue that this strongly undermines the force of Gettier's counter-examples.

In a paper co-authored by Jonathan M. Weinberg,* Shaun Nichols,* and Stephen Stich,*[2] the authors present a study that highlights differences in intuition between individuals with Western European cultural backgrounds and those with East Asian cultural backgrounds. Intuition here means an understanding that springs to mind immediately without a person having to think about the issues. The study found that westerners were much more likely than their East Asian counterparts to agree with Gettier's judgment. Again, Gettier's judgment is that the persons in his examples did not *know* the fact they accidentally got right. The authors suggest that their "data indicate that when epistemologists advert [i.e. refer] to 'our' intuitions … they are engaged in a culturally local endeavor."[3]

Other studies have suggested gender differences as well, with men much more likely than women to support Gettier's judgment.[4] Given that the audience for which Gettier was writing consisted primarily of western-educated males, it is perhaps no surprise that agreement among philosophers was mistaken for the way *all* people would see things.

Experimental philosophers, such as Ron Mallon* and Edouard Machery,* claim their results show that Gettier's thought experiments prove little. Such research is still quite new, there are questions about the methods being used, and the results are highly controversial. One reason for this is that the studies cited above[5] ask the opinion of non-philosophers. It is not clear, however, why the intuitions of non-philosophers regarding such topics ought to count for as much as those of the experts who have devoted their lives to studying the issues. One would not, after all, want to take the opinion of a non-doctor regarding the presence of a cancerous tumor as seriously as the opinion of an oncologist, who is an expert in the study of cancer.

Limitations

Edmund Gettier is all but unknown to the general public, and his work has not had an impact on the wider non-academic community. But this does not reduce the importance of what he has achieved. Gettier's article is a work of academic philosophy. Such work, as it continues to be practiced in many British and American universities today, rarely has much influence outside universities.

In the past, philosophers and their works have often had a huge impact outside philosophy. Though in the early twentieth century philosophy began to change into a formal profession, with philosophers increasingly moving to work in university departments. There they established rigorous PhD programs to standardize norms and published their work in technical peer-reviewed journals. The result has been a scholarly workforce much more specialized and isolated from the general public than it has previously been in history. This helps to explain why Gettier's paper has not received much attention from the likes of politicians or non-academic professionals.

Although Gettier's work has been investigated by highly educated specialists, and his ideas are unlikely to have an impact on everyday life in the near future, his essay has certainly contributed to debates beyond its original narrow purpose.

Gettier wrote as an epistemologist, a specialist in the branch of philosophy that investigates knowledge. Although the paper is not studied outside academia, it is certainly important to a much broader range of subjects than just this one philosophical discipline. Scholars interested in philosophical methodology, for example, have used Gettier's work to study the role played by intuition in philosophical arguments.[6] In legal circles, meanwhile, philosophers of law have used Gettier's work to investigate the connection between what we see as knowledge and trial verdicts.[7] The article's success has been far greater than anything that could have been reasonably expected.

NOTES

1   John Turri, "In Gettier's Wake," in Stephen Hetherington, ed. *Epistemology: The Key Thinkers* (London: Continuum International Publishing Group, 2012).

2   Jonathan M. Weinberg, Shaun Nichols, and Stephen Stich, "Normativity and Epistemic Intuitions," *Philosophical Topics* 29 (2001): 429–60.

3   Weinberg et al., "Normativity and Epistemic Intuitions," 454.

4   See Stephen Stich and Wesley Buckwalter, "Gender and the Philosophy Club," *The Philosophers' Magazine* 52 (2011): 60–5.

5   Weinberg et al., "Normativity and Epistemic Intuitions"; Stich and Buckwalter, "Gender and the Philosophy Club."

6   See George Bealer, "On the Possibility of Philosophical Knowledge," *Philosophical Perspectives* 10 (1996): 3–4; Weinberg et al., "Normativity and Epistemic Intuitions"; Jennifer Nagel, "Intuitions and Experiments: A Defense of the Case Method in Epistemology," *Philosophy and Phenomenological Research* 85, no. 3 (2012): 495–527.

7   See Michael Pardo, "The Gettier Problem and Legal Proof," *Legal Theory* 16, no. 1 (2010): 57.

MODULE 8
PLACE IN THE AUTHOR'S WORK

KEY POINTS

- "Is Justified True Belief Knowledge?" was Gettier's first— and only—published paper.

- Gettier was not interested in the huge discussions about the meaning of knowledge his paper set off. Nevertheless, he did have a long career teaching philosophy.

- Gettier's fame is due in large part to the class of thought experiments* that were inspired by his paper and now carry his name: so-called Gettier cases.

Positioning

Edmund Gettier's article "Is Justified True Belief Knowledge?" earned him instant and lasting respect in the philosophical community. He published his famous article early in his academic career, two years after earning his PhD from the elite Cornell University in the United States. The paper had an immediate impact, getting responses from leading philosophers within months of publication. Published in June, by December it had already generated a reply.[1] The fact that it is such a short text—just 930 words—also made it noteworthy, especially when most philosophical essays at the time stretched to 10,000 words and beyond.

What is incredible is that, by all accounts, Gettier considered his essay to be merely a minor contribution to the theory of knowledge.[2] He only published the paper because his colleagues encouraged him to do so and because he was trying to get university tenure (that is, a permanent academic job) and his chances of success would be severely reduced without published work to his name.[3]

66 Professor Gettier himself has taken no interest
in the literature which bears his name. At least, he
says he never has, and I have no reason to doubt
his word. 99

William Lycan, "On the Gettier Problem Problem"

Given the revolutionary nature of Gettier's thinking
demonstrated in this short paper, it would have been reasonable
to expect that it would have been the first of a rich body of work
by this young philosopher. However, that was not to be the case.
Amazingly, Edmund Gettier never published another paper, despite
a long career working in philosophy.

Integration

Exactly why Gettier stayed silent, given all the excitement
surrounding his work, is unclear. After he published what many
consider the most important epistemological* article of the twentieth
century, he was suddenly famous and had no need to publish again
to advance his professional standing. In 1967 he left Wayne State
University, where he was working when he wrote the article, for
the more prestigious University of Massachusetts at Amherst. Yet
it is still striking that such a famous philosopher did not publish
another original work. Longtime colleague William Lycan* says
that Gettier simply never took an interest in the debates and articles
that sprang up in response to his paper.[4] Gettier's brief university
web page does not even list epistemology—the philosophical study
of knowledge—as a research interest.[5] Perhaps he was a victim of his
own success. Perhaps his first paper cast such a long shadow that he
never felt comfortable publishing a second.

Nevertheless, Gettier went on to have a distinguished career
teaching philosophy to undergraduates and graduate students.

His courses spanned many disciplines, including philosophy of language,* metaphysics,* and modal logic.* Today he is Professor Emeritus*—meaning that, although he is retired, he continues to teach—at the University of Massachusetts.

Significance

Gettier's paper has remained a major influence ever since it was written. When the essay was first published, it forced philosophers to reconsider the justified true belief model of knowledge* and led many philosophers to change long-held theoretical ideas that were closely tied to that model. The term "Gettier Problem" quickly became a common philosophical term. It referred to the challenge of finding an analysis of knowledge that could not be overturned by so-called Gettier cases. It has been said that what is "essential to Gettier cases is that they are intended to show a disparity [a difference] between justified true belief and knowledge."[6] They are like Gettier's original examples, cases in which a person forms a true belief that is well supported by the available evidence, but where the truth of that belief is, in fact, due to chance.

Several attempts were made to solve the Gettier Problem by adding a fourth condition—on top of justification, truth, and belief—to our understanding of knowledge.[7] American philosopher Alvin Goldman,* for instance, introduced a completely new kind of analysis, in which beliefs must be formed in a particular, and more reliable, way in order to qualify as true knowledge.[8] Goldman argues that knowledge must come from a process in which a person can reliably tell the difference between what is true and what is not. By the mid-1970s, efforts to save the justified true belief theory had all but ended.

Although less attention has been paid to the Gettier Problem in recent years, Gettier himself is still famous for introducing the philosophical community to the family of thought experiments that bear his name. Gettier cases have proven to be powerful tools for challenging and changing philosophical theories.

NOTES

1   Michael Clark, "Knowledge and Grounds: A Comment on Mr. Gettier's Paper," *Analysis* 24, no. 2 (1963): 46–8.

2   Louis P. Pojman, *The Theory of Knowledge: Classical and Contemporary Readings* (Belmont, CA: Wadsworth Publishing Company, 1999), 138.

3   Pojman, *Theory of Knowledge*, 138.

4   William Lycan, "On the Gettier Problem Problem," in Stephen Hetherington, ed. *Epistemology Futures* (Oxford: Clarendon Press, 2006): 149.

5   http://www.umass.edu/philosophy/faculty/faculty-pages/gettier.htm.

6   Jennifer Nagel, Raymond Mar, and Valerie San Juan, "Authentic Gettier Cases: A Reply to Starmans and Friedman," *Cognition* 129 (2013): 668.

7   See Peter Unger's "no accident" proposal in Peter Unger, "An Analysis of Factual Knowledge," *The Journal of Philosophy* 65 (1968): 157–70, and Keith Lehrer and Thomas Paxson's "no defeat" proposal in Keith Lehrer and Thomas Paxson, "Knowledge: Undefeated Justified True Belief," *Journal of Philosophy* 66 (1969): 225–37.

8   Goldman, "Discrimination and Perceptual Knowledge," *Journal of Philosophy* 73 (1976): 771–91.

SECTION 3
IMPACT

MODULE 9
THE FIRST RESPONSES

KEY POINTS

- Gettier's article set off a storm of works on the problem of knowledge. Some philosophers criticized Gettier's work because the people in his thought experiments come to true conclusions from false starting points.

- Gettier's defenders demonstrated that it was possible to come up with counter-examples in the same style as those of Gettier that did not depend on the subjects coming to true conclusions from false starting points.

- By the mid-1970s, there was widespread agreement that Gettier had been successful in disproving the justified true belief model* of knowledge.

Criticism

When Edmund Gettier's pioneering article "Is Justified True Belief Knowledge?" first appeared in 1963, it lit a firestorm of philosophical activity. Michael Clark was the first major philosopher to respond. In a brief piece that appeared only months after Gettier's original paper, Clark proposed what has come to be called the "no-false-lemmas"* condition on knowledge.[1] Gettier's counter-examples show a person arriving—accidentally—at a true conclusion on the basis of a false statement that he or she was nonetheless justified in believing. Clark does not deny that Smith's belief is justified in Gettier's two examples, but he thinks it fails a further, previously unrecognized, condition that he proposes on knowledge. In Clark's view, Smith's belief is not "fully grounded."[2] Although each link in Smith's chain of reasoning is justified, not every link is true, resulting in a conclusion that is not fully

> " Epistemologists uniformly agree that Gettier cases at least put considerable pressure on the JTB [justified true belief] analysis of knowledge, if not refute it outright. "
>
> Steven Hales, "The Faculty of Intuition"

grounded. Conclusions made from false statements, according to Clark, can never lead to knowledge, even if they lead to justified true beliefs.

Other critics, such as Robert G. Meyers* and Kenneth Stern,* maintain that Gettier's examples fail because he has misunderstood the very nature of justification. According to him, justification is preserved by valid reasoning. He writes, "for any Proposition P, if S [somebody] is justified in believing P, and P entails [leads to] Q, and S deduces Q from P and accepts Q as a result of this deduction, then S is justified in believing Q."[3] Meyers and Stern don't accept this idea. They argue that Gettier's cases "rest on a misunderstanding about the nature of justification and are really not counter-examples" to the traditional account of knowledge after all.[4] According to them, it is impossible for an individual to have a justified belief based on evidence that is false. If Meyers and Stern are right, then Gettier's original cases do indeed fall short of genuine counter-examples to the justified true belief analysis of knowledge.

Responses

Gettier did not reply to these criticisms. He confessed he had little interest in the responses to his paper.[5] But other philosophers who were sympathetic to Gettier's work soon discovered that you could slightly change his original cases, avoid these criticisms and still disprove the justified true belief analysis of knowledge.

One of the first philosophers to come to Gettier's defense was epistemologist* Richard Feldman.* In a 1974 paper, Feldman offers another Gettier-style thought experiment.* In it, an individual arrives at a justified true belief based on *true* evidence that nonetheless fails to qualify as knowledge.[6] Then, two years later, the philosopher Alvin Goldman* wrote a paper in which he offered what has come to be seen as the model of this sort of experiment.[7]

Goldman's case can be summarized as follows:

Smith is driving through the countryside, and she sees what can only be a barn. On the basis of this visual image she forms the belief that she has seen a barn. Her belief is both true and justified. Unknown to Smith, however, she is driving through "fake barn country," and almost every single structure she sees and believes to be a barn is in fact nothing but a huge billboard painted to look like a barn. There is one, and only one, real barn in fake barn country—and it just so happens that Smith was looking at it when she formed her belief that she had seen a barn.

According to Goldman, she does not know she is looking at a barn—even when she is right.

The truth of Smith's belief is in many ways accidental. She could have easily been wrong. For this reason, her belief does not qualify as knowledge. Note, however, that the evidence upon which Smith forms the belief that she saw a barn is not false. She was in fact looking at a barn. So the objection to Gettier's original cases—that the person's belief is mistaken—is avoided. The person in Goldman's thought experiment has a justified true belief, based on true evidence, which nevertheless fails to qualify as genuine knowledge.

Conflict and Consensus

Gettier's critics raise important points about knowledge and justification by considering details that Gettier does not directly address. As the debate advanced, however, these critiques became less convincing. By the early 1970s, widespread agreement had arisen that there was a way to overcome the criticisms put forward by Clark, Meyers, and Stern. This could be done with new versions of Gettier's original counter-examples. As in Goldman's example, this is where the person does not get his or her justified true belief from a false idea.

The general agreement that arose from the dialogue of the 1960s and 1970s was that Gettier's counter-examples, and the dozens of slightly different versions they inspired, together overturned the simplistic versions of the justified true belief model of knowledge. Later thinkers in the 1980s and 1990s would propose more complex conditions on knowledge.[8] Eventually, the hunt for necessary and sufficient conditions* on knowledge declined in popularity, and epistemologists began to approach knowledge in radically new ways. For example, Timothy Williamson,* a philosopher at Oxford University, proposed a model that has come to be known as the "knowledge first" theory.[9] In this view, knowledge is already so basic that it cannot be analyzed into any more basic parts. So, according to Williamson, the project of breaking knowledge down into simpler pieces is hopeless.

NOTES

1   Michael Clark, "Knowledge and Grounds: A Comment on Mr. Gettier's Paper," *Analysis* 24, no. 2 (1963): 46–8.

2   Clark, "Knowledge and Grounds," 47.

3   Edmund L. Gettier, "Is Justified True Belief Knowledge?" *Analysis* 23, no. 6 (1963): 121.

4   Robert G. Meyers and Kenneth Stern, "Knowledge Without Paradox," *Journal of Philosophy* 70, no. 6 (1973): 149.

5   William Lycan, "On the Gettier Problem Problem," in Stephen Hetherington, ed., *Epistemology Futures* (Oxford: Clarendon Press, 2006): 149.

6   Richard Feldman, "An Alleged Defect in Gettier Counter-Examples," *Australasian Journal of Philosophy* 50 (1974): 1.

7   Alvin Goldman, "Discrimination and Perceptual Knowledge," *Journal of Philosophy* 73, (1976): 771–91.

8   See Robert Nozick, *Philosophical Explanations* (Cambridge, MA: Harvard University Press, 1981), and Ernest Sosa, "How to Defeat Opposition to Moore," *Noûs* 33 (1999): 141–53.

9   Timothy Williamson, *Knowledge and Its Limits* (Oxford: Oxford University Press, 2002).

MODULE 10
THE EVOLVING DEBATE

KEY POINTS

- Gettier's most important contribution was in introducing the philosophical community to the family of thought experiments* that bear his name.

- In an indirect way, almost every epistemologist* working after 1963 is a follower of Gettier.

- Gettier's counter-examples have proved to be so convincing that many epistemologists have now given up the idea of trying to analyze knowledge by breaking it into simpler parts.

Uses and Problems

A "Gettier case" is a thought experiment similar to the examples in Edmund Gettier's original 1963 essay "Is Justified True Belief Knowledge?". By the mid-1980s, philosophers had adapted, customized and modernized Gettier's original examples to produce more than 90 different Gettier cases.[1]

Many of these examples have become as famous as Gettier's original cases. Here are three of the best known, all paraphrased for brevity:

- In George Bealer's* example *Sheep*, Smith drives past what he takes to be a flock of sheep. He eyes one particular animal and forms the belief that there is a sheep in the pasture. He is correct, but the animal on which he bases this belief is the one sheep in a pack of white poodles. At the distance Smith is away, he cannot distinguish the poodles from the sheep. Smith does not *know* that there is a sheep in the pasture.[2]

66 The resilience of the Gettier problem suggests that it is difficult (if not impossible) to develop any explicit reductive [i.e. simplified] theory of knowledge that fully captures our actual patterns of response to particular examples.99

Jennifer Nagel, "Intuitions and Experiments"

- In Roderick Chisholm's* *Deer*, Smith looks out his window to see an animal he takes to be a deer. On this basis he forms the belief that there is a deer on his lawn. He is correct. The animal upon which he bases this belief, however, is not a deer, but a cleverly disguised dog. Yet there is, in fact, a deer on Smith's lawn, hidden behind some bushes. Smith does not *know* that there is a deer on his lawn.[3]
- In Israel Scheffler's* *Clock*, Smith checks his usually reliable analog wristwatch. The time reads 34 minutes past 11, and this is, indeed, the time. But, unknown to Smith, his watch stopped 12 hours earlier, at 34 minutes past 11. Smith does not *know* it is the time of day it actually is.[4]

Schools of Thought

Gettier's paper is purely negative. He aims to overturn the justified true belief model of knowledge, but he does not offer a theory to replace it. He never published another paper, either, so for these reasons, it is difficult to connect Gettier with any particular school of thought or to associate him with any disciples—that is, with other scholars who carried on his work.

In a sense, though, nearly all epistemologists working after 1963 are Gettier's disciples. Since his paper appeared, so-called Gettier cases have bloomed in philosophy. The three examples above, and dozens more like them, have become permanent issues of discussion for philosophy scholars. Many of the examples were originally created to disprove one or another of the updated versions of the justified true belief model. More recently, Gettier cases have been put to use outside epistemology. George Bealer, for example, uses his *Sheep* example to make a point about philosophical methodology—namely, that intuitions* are used as evidence in the discipline. The fact that there is a such large number of Gettier cases in philosophical literature shows that Gettier is still influential today, even if the cases are being used in ways Gettier did not intend or imagine. Although Gettier himself lacks clear intellectual disciples, the two cases he thought up have given birth to a rich line of philosophical thought.

In Current Scholarship

Gettier's paper continues to have an impact today. Outside epistemology, his famous cases have fueled debates in such areas as philosophy of law* and philosophical methodology.* Legal scholars have used Gettier cases to argue that juries can sometimes base their verdict on justified true belief and still reach the wrong decision. Researchers into philosophical methodology, meanwhile, have used Gettier cases to investigate the reliability of judgments based on intuition.[5]

Gettier's direct influence has most noticeably fallen inside epistemology. In many ways, his essay is the victim of its own success. The paper launched a decades-long search for a way to avoid Gettier-style counter-examples to the analysis of knowledge. Some epistemologists now regard this pursuit as a waste of energy. Gettier targeted only one specific analysis of knowledge, the justified true belief model—although, admittedly, that model is the leading analysis—but some philosophers have nevertheless drawn a wider lesson from his work. Linda Zagzebski* at the University of Oklahoma, for instance, argues that "Gettier problems are inescapable for virtually every analysis of knowledge which at least maintains that knowledge is true belief plus something else."[6] No serious analysis of knowledge will be able to avoid Gettier-style counter-examples, Zagzebski claims, because Gettier cases, by their very nature, are unavoidable. Trying not to use them is hopeless.

Zagzebski's argument has led some philosophers, most notably Timothy Williamson* at Oxford University, to give up on the project of analyzing knowledge altogether. Instead, he now takes knowledge to be a basic concept that cannot be analyzed.[7]

In a similar vein, Alvin Goldman* at Rutgers University complains that the "trouble with many philosophical treatments of knowledge is that they are inspired by Cartesian-like* conceptions of justification or vindication. There is a consequent tendency to over-intellectualize or over-rationalize the notion of knowledge."[8] ("Cartesian" relates to the ideas of the philosopher Descartes. In this context, the reference is to the desire, held by Descartes, to build knowledge from secure and infallible foundations.)

These attitudes toward knowledge suggest that Gettier's viewpoint is correct. At the same time they make it less urgent for philosophers to engage with his work.

NOTES

1 For an overview, see Robert Shope, *The Analysis of Knowing: A Decade of Research* (Princeton, NJ: Princeton University Press, 1983).

2 George Bealer, "On the Possibility of Philosophical Knowledge," *Philosophical Perspectives* 10 (1996): 3–4.

3 Roderick Chisholm, *Theory of Knowledge* (London: Prentice-Hall International, 1966).

4 Israel Scheffler, *Conditions of Knowledge: An Introduction to Epistemology and Education* (Minneapolis: University of Minnesota Press, 1965).

5 See Michael Pardo, "The Gettier Problem and Legal Proof," *Legal Theory* 16, no. 1 (2010), and Bealer "On the Possibility."

6 Linda Zagzebski, "The Inescapability of Gettier Problems," *Philosophical Quarterly* 44, no. 174 (1994): 65.

7 Timothy Williamson, *Knowledge and Its Limits* (Oxford: Oxford University Press, 2002).

8 Alvin Goldman, "Discrimination and Perceptual Knowledge," *Journal of*

MODULE 11
IMPACT AND INFLUENCE TODAY

KEY POINTS

- Gettier's two famous examples have had a major impact and have inspired thought experiments* in other areas, such as the philosophy of law.*

- Two main objections have arisen to Gettier's text. One is that the intuition* he used to reach his conclusions may not be shared across different cultures. The other is simply that using intuition is a bad method by which to overturn a model that has held for over two thousand years.

- The majority of philosophers do think Gettier's conclusions are correct and important.

Position

Edmund Gettier's "Is Justified True Belief Knowledge?" had an immediate impact. His two counter-examples marked the beginning of the end for the justified true belief (JTB) model of knowledge and the similar models that followed. Gettier's aim of disproving the JTB theory was quickly achieved, yet still his text remains part of the current intellectual debate.

Legal scholars have applied Gettier's cases to issues of philosophy of law, such as what makes a legal verdict correct or successful. A person without legal training might easily accept that a verdict is correct when a person is found guilty of a crime if, and only if, they committed it. Legal scholars, however, reject this simplistic understanding. If the accused is convicted solely on the basis of a confession obtained through the use of torture, for example, the verdict would be unjust, even if the defendant did in fact commit the crime.

❝ If we really want to know what competent speakers would say about Gettier cases, for example, let's formulate the relevant vignettes, go to McDonalds, and start asking people. One cannot tell, 'from the armchair,' what the good people dining at McDonalds will say about whether a subject in a Gettier case knows. ❞

Max Deutsch, "Experimental Philosophy and the Theory of Reference"

American legal scholar Michael Pardo* thinks that Gettier's work can help decide this question. Pardo argues for "a deeper connection between knowledge and legal proof than is generally presupposed in the legal literature."[1] To illustrate this connection, he offers a case inspired by Gettier's original counter-examples that he calls "Framed Defendant."

In Pardo's "Framed Defendant," the police arrest a driver and plant drugs in his car. He is convicted at his trial of illegal possession based solely on testimony from the officers who arrested him and on the evidence of the planted drugs. However, it turns out, the defendant *did* have illegal drugs in his car at the time that were never discovered. The verdict that the accused driver possessed drugs is therefore both true and justified (that is, the evidence at the trial was sufficient to convict the man beyond a reasonable doubt), but the truth and the justifying evidence are disconnected. The truth of the verdict (that the man was in fact carrying illegal drugs) is purely accidental.[2] Pardo claims that the court's verdict in his "Framed Defendant" case does not achieve its goals. This claim suggests that sometimes knowledge—and not merely justified true belief—is required for a verdict to be called "successful."

Pardo's work, which extends across the disciplines of philosophy and law, is an example of how Gettier's text continues to be important. Very few scholars still accept the justified true belief model of knowledge today. The essay still impacts the philosophical community outside the narrow purpose to which it was directed— disproving the JTB theory. The issues of legal theory that Pardo highlights would perhaps have gone unnoticed if Gettier had not written his groundbreaking work.

Interaction

Not all of today's philosophers think Gettier cases are useful. Their concerns can be divided into two groups. One group challenges the idea that Gettier's results are universal—that is, that they hold for all people everywhere. This group claims that so-called Gettier intuitions are not as widespread as philosophers may have thought. The other group challenges the methodology behind Gettier's results. They argue that by relying on intuitive judgment (that is, by using intuition to conclude that the persons in his two examples had justified true belief, but still did not *know* the fact in question), Gettier arrived at conclusions that were wrong.

Gettier expects his readers to share the intuitive judgment presented in the paper. Yet if they do not all share that same intuition (that is, if they feel that in fact the people in Gettier's two cases *do know* the fact in question), it is unclear whether his two cases would qualify as genuine counter-examples to the justified true belief theory of knowledge.

It should be noted that there is very little diversity within the community of philosophers today. They are mostly male, European or North American, educated, and well-to-do. Their support for Gettier, therefore, cannot be taken to represent the support of the public at large. Jonathan Weinberg,* Shaun Nichols,* and Stephen Stich* published a paper in 2001 based on surveys, that suggests Gettier intuitions are not as widespread as once thought.[3] The authors discovered important differences between the intuitions of westerners and East Asians. Those coming from a Western

European cultural background were much more likely than their East Asian counterparts to agree with Gettier's judgments. These data remain controversial, but they have complicated the way in which philosophers view Gettier's work.

The Continuing Debate

There is also a challenge today over the methods Gettier used. Some epistemologists* say they don't see a strong reason why we should give up the justified true belief theory of knowledge.[4] Intuitions—including the ones Gettier used—can be wrong. The JTB model of knowledge is clear and logical, and it was popular for thousands of years. According to this school of thought, we should not toss aside such a theory so casually. Perhaps we should let our best theories guide—and in this case, correct—our intuitions. After all, the justified true belief model is acceptable in the vast majority of cases. Indeed, what made Gettier's paper so famous, in part, is that his examples were highly imaginative and very far from ordinary.

These two challenges—"the universality objection" and "the methodological objection"—cast a serious shadow over the influence of Gettier's work. They are forcing scholars today to rethink their early understandings of Gettier's results. What is more, these questions about Gettier's work are widening the philosophical debate. What is at stake is not so much whether a particular analysis of knowledge can be saved, but the broader question of how philosophy ought to be done.

However, even these challenges themselves are highly controversial. For example, Jennifer Nagel* at the University of Toronto rejects the methodological objection. She argues that "the fact that a form of inquiry is difficult does not entail that there is anything fundamentally wrong with its methods."[5] More recently, she repeated the surveys done by Weinberg et al., but did not get the same results they reported. Nagel's work suggests that Gettier intuitions are indeed shared across cultures and that Gettier's results are as secure as they ever were.

NOTES

1   Michael Pardo, "The Gettier Problem and Legal Proof," *Legal Theory* 16, no. 1 (2010): 57.

2   Pardo, "The Gettier Problem," 50.

3   Jonathan M. Weinberg, Shaun Nichols, and Stephen Stich, "Normativity and Epistemic Intuitions," *Philosophical Topics* 29 (2001): 429–60.

4   See Brian Weatherson, "What Good Are Counterexamples?" *Philosophical Studies* 115 (2003): 1–31.

5   Jennifer Nagel, "Intuitions and Experiments: A Defense of the Case Method in Epistemology," *Philosophy and Phenomenological Research* 85, no. 3 (2012): 521.

MODULE 12
WHERE NEXT?

KEY POINTS

- The publication of "Is Justified True Belief Knowledge?" set off a wave of attempts to find a fourth condition for knowledge that would rescue the justified true belief* (JTB) notion from Gettier's brilliant attack.

- The failure so far of attempts to find the necessary and sufficient conditions* on knowledge has led many philosophers to think it is an impossible goal. Knowledge may be a basic, primitive concept that cannot be fully analyzed.

- However, Gettier's essay will continue to be read and studied. It shows how even an unknown philosopher from an unheralded institution can change philosophical history.

Potential

Edmund Gettier's 1963 article "Is Justified True Belief Knowledge?" continues to shape contemporary debates about the nature of knowledge. In response to the text, an effort was launched to save the traditional understanding of knowledge through the discovery of a fourth condition to the justified true belief analysis. Various scholars continue that effort today.

One of them is Ernest Sosa,* a philosopher at Rutgers University who maintains that knowledge *is* justified true belief with the addition of a so-called safety constraint.[1] This constraint (or limit) can be roughly put as follows: if a subject (S) were to believe a proposition (P) then in all sufficiently similar possible situations,

> ❝Almost overnight, the vast majority of epistemologists throughout the analytic community rejected what for more than two thousand years, since Plato, had been the standard analysis of the central epistemological concept, in response to a couple of imaginary examples in a three page article by someone most of them had never heard of.❞
>
> Timothy Williamson, "Armchair Philosophy, Metaphysical Modality and Counterfactual Thinking"

P would not be false. This constraint is meant to address the role of luck, which is a factor in every Gettier case.

Yet Juan Comesaña,* a philosopher at the University of Arizona, has offered a counter-example to Sosa's analysis in the spirit of Gettier's original thought experiments.*[2] Unlike Gettier's original thought experiments, which challenged the sufficiency of the justified true belief model, Comesaña's case is a counter-example to the necessity of Sosa's analysis. Although the details of Comesaña's case are extremely complex, the important point is that the back-and-forth search for the elusive "fourth condition" on knowledge, which so dominated epistemology* immediately after Gettier published his article, has not completely faded away. Whether these are the final sparks of a dying enterprise or the flames that will rekindle the old project remains to be seen.

Future Directions

A growing number of philosophers today question the wisdom of joining projects of the type that were designed to break down an understanding of what knowledge is. William Ramsey,* a philosopher at the University of Nevada, Las Vegas, regrets the "failure of analytic philosophy to produce an uncontroversial, completely satisfactory analysis" for the vast majority of concepts it has tried to analyze.[3] Ramsey says that notions like "knowledge" are not black-and-white issues. Rather, they are complex, nuanced, and subtle, and the hope of finding a simple set of necessary and sufficient conditions* for such concepts is unrealistic. Philosopher Timothy Williamson,* one of the world's leading epistemologists, asserts that all attempts to find a foolproof formula for such concepts have failed. He argues that this failure suggests that attempts to come up with a complete analysis of knowledge are "misconceived."[4] According to Williamson, knowledge is a basic, primitive concept that cannot be fully analyzed.

If this change in philosophical thinking (the acceptance of the idea that knowledge cannot be fully analyzed) might impact the future significance of Gettier's paper, it is unclear as to exactly how. Gettier, of course, did not offer a fourth condition on knowledge, so it is not his project that has failed. Yet counter-examples to the justified true belief model of knowledge are only important as long as epistemologists believe that a new and more successful model can be found to replace the JTB one. If the justified true belief theory of knowledge comes to be regarded as doomed and with no future, then it will no longer be necessary to give Gettier's counter-examples any further consideration.

Summary

Edmund Gettier's "Is Justified True Belief Knowledge?" brought about a rare event in philosophy: a wholesale (one might well say devastating) shift in viewpoint over a very short period of time.

Gettier's paper is proof of the power of raw ideas in philosophy. Throughout history, philosophers have tried to discover eternal truths about the universe in which we live. Such truths are supposed to be independent of faith, culture, personality, and prejudice. All too often, however, philosophers allow their judgment of truth to be influenced by some political, socio-economic, or personal bias. It is refreshing, then, to find an event in the history of philosophy in which an unknown philosopher from an uncelebrated institution— an individual the philosophical community had every reason to ignore—challenges a long-held position and succeeds so dramatically. Put simply, Gettier's ideas are more important than their author.

If Edmund Gettier's paper has been called "extremely unusual" and "an anomaly,"[5] these adjectives are not meant to be disapproving and dismissive. What is unusual about Gettier's writing is that it is so clear, concise, and persuasive. What is equally unusual is that the quality and importance of the text was recognized immediately. Rarely has so short a text cast such a long shadow.

NOTES

1   Ernest Sosa. "How to Defeat Opposition to Moore," *Noûs* 33, no. 13 (1999): 141–53.

2   Juan Comesaña. "Unsafe Knowledge," *Synthese* 146, no. 3 (2005): 395–404.

3   William Ramsey, "Prototypes and Conceptual Analysis," in Michael DePaul and William Ramsey, eds., *Rethinking Intuition: The Psychology of Intuition and Its Role in Philosophical Inquiry* (Lanham, MD: Rowman and Littlefield, 1998), 174.

4   Timothy Phil, *Knowledge and Its Limits* (Oxford: Oxford University Press, 2002), 50.

5   Herman Cappelen, *Philosophy without Intuitions* (Oxford: Oxford University Press, 2012), 194.

GLOSSARIES

GLOSSARY OF TERMS

Cartesian doubt: a form of methodological skepticism developed by the French philosopher René Descartes.* It aims to use doubt as a means to understand knowledge by finding things that cannot be doubted.

Conceptual analysis: the process of breaking down a concept of interest into simpler parts so that its logical structure is displayed.

Disjunction: a sentence in which two or more clauses (called the "disjuncts") are connected by the word "or." A disjunction is true if and only if one or more of the disjuncts is true.

Epistemology: the systematic philosophical examination of knowledge and related concepts, like justification and rationality. An epistemologist is a philosopher who specializes in this branch of philosophy.

Ethics: the philosophical study of how people ought to live their lives.

Experimental philosophy: a new and controversial sub-discipline of philosophy. Experimental philosophers collect and analyze surveys and other data concerning the intuitions* that non-philosophers have about important philosophical thought experiments.

Intuition: an immediate perception of the truth of a matter that does not rely on any particular reasoning and may or may not prove to be true.

Justified True Belief model of knowledge: a model that states a belief is justified if it is well supported by the available evidence. According to this model, a belief rises to the level of knowledge when (and only when) it is both true and justified. The justified true belief account first appears in Plato's dialogues the *Theaetetus* and the *Meno* of the fourth century B.C.E.

Lemma: a step in an argument.

Metaphysics: the philosophical investigation into the fundamental nature of reality.

Modal logic: a branch of formal logic that studies the deductive behavior of possibility and necessity claims.

Necessary and sufficient conditions: a necessary condition is a condition that must be met in order for some further condition to hold. A sufficient condition is one that guarantees that the further condition will hold.

Philosophical methodology: the philosophical study of philosophy itself. The field of philosophical methodology attempts to articulate and evaluate the aim(s) of philosophy, the value(s) of philosophy, and the method(s) of philosophy. One striking feature of contemporary philosophical methodology is the attention it devotes to the study of philosophical intuitions.*

Philosophy of language: a branch of philosophy that investigates how written words and spoken language come to have the meanings that they do and how they come to represent the world.

Philosophy of law: a branch of philosophy that examines the abstract nature of legal systems. Questions asked typically include "What makes a verdict correct?" and "What is the connection between law and morality?"

Professor Emeritus: a retired professor who is still active in his or her former department.

Proposition: in philosophy, a proposition is a claim—true or false—that can be expressed in sentences.

Thought experiment: an imaginary scenario which is described in order to invoke an intuition* or demonstrate a philosophical point.

PEOPLE MENTIONED IN THE TEXT

George Bealer is Professor Emeritus of philosophy at Yale University. Bealer writes on logic, philosophy of language, philosophical methodology, and metaphysics.

Max Black (1909–1988) was a British-American philosopher, who worked in the philosophy of language, the philosophy of mind, and metaphysics. He is perhaps best known for his work in the field of the metaphysics of identity.

Herman Cappelen (b. 1967) is a Norwegian philosopher currently affiliated with the University of St. Andrews. Cappelen works in the fields of philosophy of language, epistemology, and philosophical methodology.

Roderick Chisholm (1916–99) was an American philosopher affiliated with Brown University. He was noted for his research in epistemology and metaphysics.

Michael Clark is editor of the journal *Analysis*. He has published widely in a variety of areas, including philosophical logic and the philosophy of law.

Juan Comesaña is professor of philosophy at the University of Arizona. Comesaña writes mainly in epistemology, but also in metaphysics and ethics.

René Descartes (1596–1650) was a seventeenth-century French philosopher and mathematician. He is most famous for his *Meditations on First Philosophy*.

Max Deutsch is an associate professor of philosophy at the University of Hong Kong. He studies philosophy of language and philosophical methodology.

Richard Feldman (b. 1948) is an American philosopher and dean of the College of Arts, Sciences, and Engineering at the University of Rochester. He works primarily in epistemology.

Alvin Goldman (b. 1938) is an American philosopher at Rutgers University, who has published widely in epistemology, metaphysics, and cognitive science.

Keith Lehrer (b. 1936) is Professor Emeritus* of philosophy at the University of Arizona. He is best known for his work in epistemology, and especially for his work in the philosophy of justification.

William Lycan (b. 1945) is an American philosopher affiliated with the University of North Carolina at Chapel Hill. He is best known for his work in the philosophy of mind.

Edouard Machery is professor of philosophy at the University of Pittsburgh.

Norman Malcolm (1911–90) was an American philosopher affiliated with Cornell University. He worked in the philosophy of mind and the philosophy of language, and advocated common sense approaches to philosophical problems.

Ron Mallon is associate professor of philosophy at Washington University in St. Louis.

Robert G. Meyers is Emeritus Professor of philosophy at the Department of Philosophy, University at Albany, New York (SUNY).

Jennifer Nagel is associate professor of philosophy at the University of Toronto. She writes primarily on epistemology.

Shaun Nichols is a philosopher at the University of Arizona who co-authored a 2001 study into differences in intuition between individuals with Western European cultural backgrounds and individuals with East Asian cultural backgrounds.

Michael Pardo is an American legal scholar. He is director of the University of Alabama's Program on Cross-Disciplinary Legal Studies.

Alvin Plantinga (b. 1932) is an American philosopher affiliated with the University of Notre Dame in Indiana. He is best known for his work in the philosophy of religion, and especially for his defense of a traditional Christian worldview.

Plato (427–347 B.C.E.**)** was an ancient Athenian philosopher and founder of the first institute of higher learning in the western world, the Academy. He composed more than two dozen philosophical dialogues, most notably *The Republic*. The justified true belief account first appears in Plato's dialogues the *Theaetetus* and the *Meno*.

Willard Van Orman Quine (1908–2000) was an American philosopher and logician affiliated with Harvard University. He is known for attacking the alleged distinction between analytic statements and synthetic statements in works such as *Word and Object*.

William Ramsey is professor of philosophy at the University of Nevada at Las Vegas. He writes in philosophy of mind and philosophy of science.

Bertrand Russell (1872–1970) was a British philosopher and early champion of analytic approaches to philosophical problems, as well as a leading philosopher and public intellectual for more than five decades. Russell published *The Problems of Philosophy*, an accessible and influential introduction to philosophy, in 1912.

Israel Scheffler (1923–2014) was an American philosopher affiliated with Harvard University. He wrote on the philosophy of science and philosophy of education.

Ernest Sosa (b. 1940) is a Cuban American philosopher affiliated most closely with Brown University, though since 2007 he has been at Rutgers University full-time. Sosa has published dozens of important works in epistemology.

Kenneth Stern (1930–2011) studied at City College, New York, Yale University and Oxford University, and taught at NYU and Smith College, among other institutions, before taking a position in the philosophy department at the University of Albany, retiring in 2000.

Stephen Stich (b. 1943) is a philosopher at Rutgers University, best known for his groundbreaking work in the philosophy of mind. He has also contributed to the burgeoning field of experimental philosophy, and co-authored a 2001 study into differences in intuition between individuals with Western European cultural backgrounds and individuals with East Asian cultural backgrounds..

Jonathan M. Weinberg is a philosopher at the University of Arizona, and he co-authored a 2001 study into differences in intuition between individuals with Western European cultural backgrounds and individuals with East Asian cultural backgrounds.

Timothy Williamson (b. 1955) is a British philosopher at Oxford University. He has made important contributions to the philosophy of language, the philosophy of knowledge, and the philosophy of philosophy.

Ludwig Wittgenstein (1889–1951) was an Austrian-British philosopher affiliated with Cambridge University. He was a major philosophical figure in the early twentieth century, making important contributions to the philosophy of mathematics and the philosophy of logic.

Linda Zagzebski (b. 1946) is an American philosopher at the University of Oklahoma. Zagzebski works primarily in ethics and epistemology.

WORKS CITED

WORKS CITED

Ayer, A. J. *The Problem of Knowledge.* London: Macmillan, 1956.

Bealer, George. "On the Possibility of Philosophical Knowledge." *Philosophical Perspectives* 10 (1996): 1–34.

BonJour, Laurence. "The Myth of Knowledge." *Philosophical Perspectives* 24 (2010): 57–83.

Cappelen, Herman. *Philosophy without Intuitions*. Oxford: Oxford University Press, 2012.

Chisholm, Roderick M. *Perceiving: a Philosophical Study*. Ithaca, NY: Cornell University Press, 1957.

———. *Theory of Knowledge*. London: Prentice-Hall International, 1966.

Clark, Michael. "Knowledge and Grounds: A Comment on Mr. Gettier's Paper." *Analysis* 24, no. 2 (1963): 46–8.

Comesaña, Juan. "Unsafe Knowledge." *Synthese*, 146, no. 3 (2005): 395–404.

Descartes, René. *Philosophical Writings of Descartes*, 3 vols., trans. John Cottingham, Robert Stoothoff, Dugald Murdoch, and Anthony Kenny. Cambridge: Cambridge University Press, 1984–91.

Deutsch, Max. "Experimental Philosophy and the Theory of Reference." *Mind & Language* 24, no. 4 (2009): 445–66.

———. "Intuitions, Counter-Examples, and Experimental Philosophy." *Review of Philosophy and Psychology* 1, no. 3 (2010): 447–60.

Feldman, Richard. "An Alleged Defect in Gettier Counter-Examples." *Australasian Journal of Philosophy* 50 (1974): 1.

Gettier, Edmund L. "Is Justified True Belief Knowledge?" *Analysis* 23, no. 6 (1963): 121–3.

Goldman, Alvin. "Discrimination and Perceptual Knowledge." *Journal of Philosophy* 73 (1976): 771–91.

Hales, Steven. "The Faculty of Intuition." *Analytic Philosophy,* 53 no. 2 (2012): 180–207.

Kratzer, Angelika. "Facts: Particulars or Information Units?" *Linguistics and Philosophy* 25 (2002): 655–70.

Lehrer, Keith and Thomas Paxson. "Knowledge: Undefeated Justified True Belief." *Journal of Philosophy* 66 (1969): 225–37.

Lycan, William. "On the Gettier Problem Problem." In *Epistemology Futures*, edited by Stephen Hetherington. Oxford: Clarendon Press, 2006.

Meyers, Robert G. and Kenneth Stern. "Knowledge Without Paradox." *Journal of Philosophy* 70, no. 6 (1973): 147–60.

Nagel, Jennifer. "Intuitions and Experiments: A Defense of the Case Method in Epistemology." *Philosophy and Phenomenological Research* 85, no 3 (2012): 495–527.

Nagel, Jennifer, Raymond Mar, and Valerie San Juan. "Authentic Gettier Cases: A Reply to Starmans and Friedman." *Cognition* 129 (2013): 666–9.

Pardo, Michael. "The Gettier Problem and Legal Proof." *Legal Theory* 16, no. 1 (2010): 37–57.

Plato. *Complete Works*. Edited by John M. Cooper. Indianapolis: Hackett Publishing Company, 1997.

Pojman, Louis P. (ed.) *The Theory of Knowledge: Classical and Contemporary Readings*. Belmont, CA: Wadsworth Publishing Company, 1999.

Ramsey, William. "Prototypes and Conceptual Analysis." In *Rethinking Intuition: The Psychology of Intuition and Its Role in Philosophical Inquiry*, edited by Michael DePaul and William Ramsey. Lanham, MD: Rowman & Littlefield, 1998.

Russell, Bertrand. *The Problems of Philosophy*. Oxford: Oxford University Press, 1912/1959.

Scheffler, Israel. *Conditions of Knowledge: An Introduction to Epistemology and Education*. Minneapolis: University of Minnesota Press, 1965.

Shope, Robert. *The Analysis of Knowing: A Decade of Research*. Princeton, NJ: Princeton University Press, 1983.

———. "Conditions and Analyses of Knowing." In *The Oxford Handbook of Epistemology.* Oxford: Oxford University Press, 2002.

Sosa, Ernest. "How to Defeat Opposition to Moore." *Noûs* 33, no. 13 (1999): 141–53.

Stich, Stephen and Wesley Buckwalter. "Gender and the Philosophy Club." *The Philosophers' Magazine* 52 (2011): 60–5.

Turri, John. "In Gettier's Wake." In *Epistemology: The Key Thinkers*, edited by Stephen Hetherington. London: Continuum International Publishing Group, 2012.

Unger, Peter. "An Analysis of Factual Knowledge." *Journal of Philosophy* 65 (1968): 157–70.

Weatherson, Brian. "What Good Are Counterexamples?" *Philosophical Studies* 115 (2003): 1–31.

Weinberg, Jonathan M., Shaun Nichols, and Stephen Stich. "Normativity and Epistemic Intuitions." *Philosophical Topics* 29 (2001): 429–60.

Williamson, Timothy. "Armchair Philosophy, Metaphysical Modality, and Counterfactual Thinking." *Proceedings of the Aristotelian Society* 105, no. 1 (2005): 1–23.

———. *Knowledge and Its Limits*. Oxford: Oxford University Press, 2002.

Zagzebski, Linda. "The Inescapability of Gettier Problems." *Philosophical Quarterly* 44, no. 174 (1994): 65–73.

THE MACAT LIBRARY
BY DISCIPLINE

AFRICANA STUDIES

Chinua Achebe's *An Image of Africa: Racism in Conrad's Heart of Darkness*
W. E. B. Du Bois's *The Souls of Black Folk*
Zora Neale Huston's *Characteristics of Negro Expression*
Martin Luther King Jr's *Why We Can't Wait*
Toni Morrison's *Playing in the Dark: Whiteness in the American Literary Imagination*

ANTHROPOLOGY

Arjun Appadurai's *Modernity at Large: Cultural Dimensions of Globalisation*
Philippe Ariès's *Centuries of Childhood*
Franz Boas's *Race, Language and Culture*
Kim Chan & Renée Mauborgne's *Blue Ocean Strategy*
Jared Diamond's *Guns, Germs & Steel: the Fate of Human Societies*
Jared Diamond's *Collapse: How Societies Choose to Fail or Survive*
E. E. Evans-Pritchard's *Witchcraft, Oracles and Magic Among the Azande*
James Ferguson's *The Anti-Politics Machine*
Clifford Geertz's *The Interpretation of Cultures*
David Graeber's *Debt: the First 5000 Years*
Karen Ho's *Liquidated: An Ethnography of Wall Street*
Geert Hofstede's *Culture's Consequences: Comparing Values, Behaviors, Institutes and Organizations across Nations*
Claude Lévi-Strauss's *Structural Anthropology*
Jay Macleod's *Ain't No Makin' It: Aspirations and Attainment in a Low-Income Neighborhood*
Saba Mahmood's *The Politics of Piety: The Islamic Revival and the Feminist Subject*
Marcel Mauss's *The Gift*

BUSINESS

Jean Lave & Etienne Wenger's *Situated Learning*
Theodore Levitt's *Marketing Myopia*
Burton G. Malkiel's *A Random Walk Down Wall Street*
Douglas McGregor's *The Human Side of Enterprise*
Michael Porter's *Competitive Strategy: Creating and Sustaining Superior Performance*
John Kotter's *Leading Change*
C. K. Prahalad & Gary Hamel's *The Core Competence of the Corporation*

CRIMINOLOGY

Michelle Alexander's *The New Jim Crow: Mass Incarceration in the Age of Colorblindness*
Michael R. Gottfredson & Travis Hirschi's *A General Theory of Crime*
Richard Herrnstein & Charles A. Murray's *The Bell Curve: Intelligence and Class Structure in American Life*
Elizabeth Loftus's *Eyewitness Testimony*
Jay Macleod's *Ain't No Makin' It: Aspirations and Attainment in a Low-Income Neighborhood*
Philip Zimbardo's *The Lucifer Effect*

ECONOMICS

Janet Abu-Lughod's *Before European Hegemony*
Ha-Joon Chang's *Kicking Away the Ladder*
David Brion Davis's *The Problem of Slavery in the Age of Revolution*
Milton Friedman's *The Role of Monetary Policy*
Milton Friedman's *Capitalism and Freedom*
David Graeber's *Debt: the First 5000 Years*
Friedrich Hayek's *The Road to Serfdom*
Karen Ho's *Liquidated: An Ethnography of Wall Street*

John Maynard Keynes's *The General Theory of Employment, Interest and Money*
Charles P. Kindleberger's *Manias, Panics and Crashes*
Robert Lucas's *Why Doesn't Capital Flow from Rich to Poor Countries?*
Burton G. Malkiel's *A Random Walk Down Wall Street*
Thomas Robert Malthus's *An Essay on the Principle of Population*
Karl Marx's *Capital*
Thomas Piketty's *Capital in the Twenty-First Century*
Amartya Sen's *Development as Freedom*
Adam Smith's *The Wealth of Nations*
Nassim Nicholas Taleb's *The Black Swan: The Impact of the Highly Improbable*
Amos Tversky's & Daniel Kahneman's *Judgment under Uncertainty: Heuristics and Biases*
Mahbub Ul Haq's *Reflections on Human Development*
Max Weber's *The Protestant Ethic and the Spirit of Capitalism*

FEMINISM AND GENDER STUDIES

Judith Butler's *Gender Trouble*
Simone De Beauvoir's *The Second Sex*
Michel Foucault's *History of Sexuality*
Betty Friedan's *The Feminine Mystique*
Saba Mahmood's *The Politics of Piety: The Islamic Revival and the Feminist Subject*
Joan Wallach Scott's *Gender and the Politics of History*
Mary Wollstonecraft's *A Vindication of the Rights of Woman*
Virginia Woolf's *A Room of One's Own*

GEOGRAPHY

The Brundtland Report's *Our Common Future*
Rachel Carson's *Silent Spring*
Charles Darwin's *On the Origin of Species*
James Ferguson's *The Anti-Politics Machine*
Jane Jacobs's *The Death and Life of Great American Cities*
James Lovelock's *Gaia: A New Look at Life on Earth*
Amartya Sen's *Development as Freedom*
Mathis Wackernagel & William Rees's *Our Ecological Footprint*

HISTORY

Janet Abu-Lughod's *Before European Hegemony*
Benedict Anderson's *Imagined Communities*
Bernard Bailyn's *The Ideological Origins of the American Revolution*
Hanna Batatu's *The Old Social Classes And The Revolutionary Movements Of Iraq*
Christopher Browning's *Ordinary Men: Reserve Police Batallion 101 and the Final Solution in Poland*
Edmund Burke's *Reflections on the Revolution in France*
William Cronon's *Nature's Metropolis: Chicago And The Great West*
Alfred W. Crosby's *The Columbian Exchange*
Hamid Dabashi's *Iran: A People Interrupted*
David Brion Davis's *The Problem of Slavery in the Age of Revolution*
Nathalie Zemon Davis's *The Return of Martin Guerre*
Jared Diamond's *Guns, Germs & Steel: the Fate of Human Societies*
Frank Dikotter's *Mao's Great Famine*
John W Dower's *War Without Mercy: Race And Power In The Pacific War*
W. E. B. Du Bois's *The Souls of Black Folk*
Richard J. Evans's *In Defence of History*
Lucien Febvre's *The Problem of Unbelief in the 16th Century*
Sheila Fitzpatrick's *Everyday Stalinism*

Eric Foner's *Reconstruction: America's Unfinished Revolution, 1863-1877*
Michel Foucault's *Discipline and Punish*
Michel Foucault's *History of Sexuality*
Francis Fukuyama's *The End of History and the Last Man*
John Lewis Gaddis's *We Now Know: Rethinking Cold War History*
Ernest Gellner's *Nations and Nationalism*
Eugene Genovese's *Roll, Jordan, Roll: The World the Slaves Made*
Carlo Ginzburg's *The Night Battles*
Daniel Goldhagen's *Hitler's Willing Executioners*
Jack Goldstone's *Revolution and Rebellion in the Early Modern World*
Antonio Gramsci's *The Prison Notebooks*
Alexander Hamilton, John Jay & James Madison's *The Federalist Papers*
Christopher Hill's *The World Turned Upside Down*
Carole Hillenbrand's *The Crusades: Islamic Perspectives*
Thomas Hobbes's *Leviathan*
Eric Hobsbawm's *The Age Of Revolution*
John A. Hobson's *Imperialism: A Study*
Albert Hourani's *History of the Arab Peoples*
Samuel P. Huntington's *The Clash of Civilizations and the Remaking of World Order*
C. L. R. James's *The Black Jacobins*
Tony Judt's *Postwar: A History of Europe Since 1945*
Ernst Kantorowicz's *The King's Two Bodies: A Study in Medieval Political Theology*
Paul Kennedy's *The Rise and Fall of the Great Powers*
Ian Kershaw's *The "Hitler Myth": Image and Reality in the Third Reich*
John Maynard Keynes's *The General Theory of Employment, Interest and Money*
Charles P. Kindleberger's *Manias, Panics and Crashes*
Martin Luther King Jr's *Why We Can't Wait*
Henry Kissinger's *World Order: Reflections on the Character of Nations and the Course of History*
Thomas Kuhn's *The Structure of Scientific Revolutions*
Georges Lefebvre's *The Coming of the French Revolution*
John Locke's *Two Treatises of Government*
Niccolò Machiavelli's *The Prince*
Thomas Robert Malthus's *An Essay on the Principle of Population*
Mahmood Mamdani's *Citizen and Subject: Contemporary Africa And The Legacy Of Late Colonialism*
Karl Marx's *Capital*
Stanley Milgram's *Obedience to Authority*
John Stuart Mill's *On Liberty*
Thomas Paine's *Common Sense*
Thomas Paine's *Rights of Man*
Geoffrey Parker's *Global Crisis: War, Climate Change and Catastrophe in the Seventeenth Century*
Jonathan Riley-Smith's *The First Crusade and the Idea of Crusading*
Jean-Jacques Rousseau's *The Social Contract*
Joan Wallach Scott's *Gender and the Politics of History*
Theda Skocpol's *States and Social Revolutions*
Adam Smith's *The Wealth of Nations*
Timothy Snyder's *Bloodlands: Europe Between Hitler and Stalin*
Sun Tzu's *The Art of War*
Keith Thomas's *Religion and the Decline of Magic*
Thucydides's *The History of the Peloponnesian War*
Frederick Jackson Turner's *The Significance of the Frontier in American History*
Odd Arne Westad's *The Global Cold War: Third World Interventions And The Making Of Our Times*

The Macat Library By Discipline

LITERATURE

Chinua Achebe's *An Image of Africa: Racism in Conrad's Heart of Darkness*
Roland Barthes's *Mythologies*
Homi K. Bhabha's *The Location of Culture*
Judith Butler's *Gender Trouble*
Simone De Beauvoir's *The Second Sex*
Ferdinand De Saussure's *Course in General Linguistics*
T. S. Eliot's *The Sacred Wood: Essays on Poetry and Criticism*
Zora Neale Huston's *Characteristics of Negro Expression*
Toni Morrison's *Playing in the Dark: Whiteness in the American Literary Imagination*
Edward Said's *Orientalism*
Gayatri Chakravorty Spivak's *Can the Subaltern Speak?*
Mary Wollstonecraft's *A Vindication of the Rights of Women*
Virginia Woolf's *A Room of One's Own*

PHILOSOPHY

Elizabeth Anscombe's *Modern Moral Philosophy*
Hannah Arendt's *The Human Condition*
Aristotle's *Metaphysics*
Aristotle's *Nicomachean Ethics*
Edmund Gettier's *Is Justified True Belief Knowledge?*
Georg Wilhelm Friedrich Hegel's *Phenomenology of Spirit*
David Hume's *Dialogues Concerning Natural Religion*
David Hume's *The Enquiry for Human Understanding*
Immanuel Kant's *Religion within the Boundaries of Mere Reason*
Immanuel Kant's *Critique of Pure Reason*
Søren Kierkegaard's *The Sickness Unto Death*
Søren Kierkegaard's *Fear and Trembling*
C. S. Lewis's *The Abolition of Man*
Alasdair MacIntyre's *After Virtue*
Marcus Aurelius's *Meditations*
Friedrich Nietzsche's *On the Genealogy of Morality*
Friedrich Nietzsche's *Beyond Good and Evil*
Plato's *Republic*
Plato's *Symposium*
Jean-Jacques Rousseau's *The Social Contract*
Gilbert Ryle's *The Concept of Mind*
Baruch Spinoza's *Ethics*
Sun Tzu's *The Art of War*
Ludwig Wittgenstein's *Philosophical Investigations*

POLITICS

Benedict Anderson's *Imagined Communities*
Aristotle's *Politics*
Bernard Bailyn's *The Ideological Origins of the American Revolution*
Edmund Burke's *Reflections on the Revolution in France*
John C. Calhoun's *A Disquisition on Government*
Ha-Joon Chang's *Kicking Away the Ladder*
Hamid Dabashi's *Iran: A People Interrupted*
Hamid Dabashi's *Theology of Discontent: The Ideological Foundation of the Islamic Revolution in Iran*
Robert Dahl's *Democracy and its Critics*
Robert Dahl's *Who Governs?*
David Brion Davis's *The Problem of Slavery in the Age of Revolution*

Alexis De Tocqueville's *Democracy in America*
James Ferguson's *The Anti-Politics Machine*
Frank Dikotter's *Mao's Great Famine*
Sheila Fitzpatrick's *Everyday Stalinism*
Eric Foner's *Reconstruction: America's Unfinished Revolution, 1863-1877*
Milton Friedman's *Capitalism and Freedom*
Francis Fukuyama's *The End of History and the Last Man*
John Lewis Gaddis's *We Now Know: Rethinking Cold War History*
Ernest Gellner's *Nations and Nationalism*
David Graeber's *Debt: the First 5000 Years*
Antonio Gramsci's *The Prison Notebooks*
Alexander Hamilton, John Jay & James Madison's *The Federalist Papers*
Friedrich Hayek's *The Road to Serfdom*
Christopher Hill's *The World Turned Upside Down*
Thomas Hobbes's *Leviathan*
John A. Hobson's *Imperialism: A Study*
Samuel P. Huntington's *The Clash of Civilizations and the Remaking of World Order*
Tony Judt's *Postwar: A History of Europe Since 1945*
David C. Kang's *China Rising: Peace, Power and Order in East Asia*
Paul Kennedy's *The Rise and Fall of Great Powers*
Robert Keohane's *After Hegemony*
Martin Luther King Jr.'s *Why We Can't Wait*
Henry Kissinger's *World Order: Reflections on the Character of Nations and the Course of History*
John Locke's *Two Treatises of Government*
Niccolò Machiavelli's *The Prince*
Thomas Robert Malthus's *An Essay on the Principle of Population*
Mahmood Mamdani's *Citizen and Subject: Contemporary Africa And The Legacy Of Late Colonialism*
Karl Marx's *Capital*
John Stuart Mill's *On Liberty*
John Stuart Mill's *Utilitarianism*
Hans Morgenthau's *Politics Among Nations*
Thomas Paine's *Common Sense*
Thomas Paine's *Rights of Man*
Thomas Piketty's *Capital in the Twenty-First Century*
Robert D. Putman's *Bowling Alone*
John Rawls's *Theory of Justice*
Jean-Jacques Rousseau's *The Social Contract*
Theda Skocpol's *States and Social Revolutions*
Adam Smith's *The Wealth of Nations*
Sun Tzu's *The Art of War*
Henry David Thoreau's *Civil Disobedience*
Thucydides's *The History of the Peloponnesian War*
Kenneth Waltz's *Theory of International Politics*
Max Weber's *Politics as a Vocation*
Odd Arne Westad's *The Global Cold War: Third World Interventions And The Making Of Our Times*

POSTCOLONIAL STUDIES

Roland Barthes's *Mythologies*
Frantz Fanon's *Black Skin, White Masks*
Homi K. Bhabha's *The Location of Culture*
Gustavo Gutiérrez's *A Theology of Liberation*
Edward Said's *Orientalism*
Gayatri Chakravorty Spivak's *Can the Subaltern Speak?*

The Macat Library By Discipline

PSYCHOLOGY

Gordon Allport's *The Nature of Prejudice*
Alan Baddeley & Graham Hitch's *Aggression: A Social Learning Analysis*
Albert Bandura's *Aggression: A Social Learning Analysis*
Leon Festinger's *A Theory of Cognitive Dissonance*
Sigmund Freud's *The Interpretation of Dreams*
Betty Friedan's *The Feminine Mystique*
Michael R. Gottfredson & Travis Hirschi's *A General Theory of Crime*
Eric Hoffer's *The True Believer: Thoughts on the Nature of Mass Movements*
William James's *Principles of Psychology*
Elizabeth Loftus's *Eyewitness Testimony*
A. H. Maslow's *A Theory of Human Motivation*
Stanley Milgram's *Obedience to Authority*
Steven Pinker's *The Better Angels of Our Nature*
Oliver Sacks's *The Man Who Mistook His Wife For a Hat*
Richard Thaler & Cass Sunstein's *Nudge: Improving Decisions About Health, Wealth and Happiness*
Amos Tversky's *Judgment under Uncertainty: Heuristics and Biases*
Philip Zimbardo's *The Lucifer Effect*

SCIENCE

Rachel Carson's *Silent Spring*
William Cronon's *Nature's Metropolis: Chicago And The Great West*
Alfred W. Crosby's *The Columbian Exchange*
Charles Darwin's *On the Origin of Species*
Richard Dawkin's *The Selfish Gene*
Thomas Kuhn's *The Structure of Scientific Revolutions*
Geoffrey Parker's *Global Crisis: War, Climate Change and Catastrophe in the Seventeenth Century*
Mathis Wackernagel & William Rees's *Our Ecological Footprint*

SOCIOLOGY

Michelle Alexander's *The New Jim Crow: Mass Incarceration in the Age of Colorblindness*
Gordon Allport's *The Nature of Prejudice*
Albert Bandura's *Aggression: A Social Learning Analysis*
Hanna Batatu's *The Old Social Classes And The Revolutionary Movements Of Iraq*
Ha-Joon Chang's *Kicking Away the Ladder*
W. E. B. Du Bois's *The Souls of Black Folk*
Émile Durkheim's *On Suicide*
Frantz Fanon's *Black Skin, White Masks*
Frantz Fanon's *The Wretched of the Earth*
Eric Foner's *Reconstruction: America's Unfinished Revolution, 1863-1877*
Eugene Genovese's *Roll, Jordan, Roll: The World the Slaves Made*
Jack Goldstone's *Revolution and Rebellion in the Early Modern World*
Antonio Gramsci's *The Prison Notebooks*
Richard Herrnstein & Charles A Murray's *The Bell Curve: Intelligence and Class Structure in American Life*
Eric Hoffer's *The True Believer: Thoughts on the Nature of Mass Movements*
Jane Jacobs's *The Death and Life of Great American Cities*
Robert Lucas's *Why Doesn't Capital Flow from Rich to Poor Countries?*
Jay Macleod's *Ain't No Makin' It: Aspirations and Attainment in a Low Income Neighborhood*
Elaine May's *Homeward Bound: American Families in the Cold War Era*
Douglas McGregor's *The Human Side of Enterprise*
C. Wright Mills's *The Sociological Imagination*

Thomas Piketty's *Capital in the Twenty-First Century*
Robert D. Putman's *Bowling Alone*
David Riesman's *The Lonely Crowd: A Study of the Changing American Character*
Edward Said's *Orientalism*
Joan Wallach Scott's *Gender and the Politics of History*
Theda Skocpol's *States and Social Revolutions*
Max Weber's *The Protestant Ethic and the Spirit of Capitalism*

THEOLOGY

Augustine's *Confessions*
Benedict's *Rule of St Benedict*
Gustavo Gutiérrez's *A Theology of Liberation*
Carole Hillenbrand's *The Crusades: Islamic Perspectives*
David Hume's *Dialogues Concerning Natural Religion*
Immanuel Kant's *Religion within the Boundaries of Mere Reason*
Ernst Kantorowicz's *The King's Two Bodies: A Study in Medieval Political Theology*
Søren Kierkegaard's *The Sickness Unto Death*
C. S. Lewis's *The Abolition of Man*
Saba Mahmood's *The Politics of Piety: The Islamic Revival and the Feminist Subject*
Baruch Spinoza's *Ethics*
Keith Thomas's *Religion and the Decline of Magic*

COMING SOON

Chris Argyris's *The Individual and the Organisation*
Seyla Benhabib's *The Rights of Others*
Walter Benjamin's *The Work Of Art in the Age of Mechanical Reproduction*
John Berger's *Ways of Seeing*
Pierre Bourdieu's *Outline of a Theory of Practice*
Mary Douglas's *Purity and Danger*
Roland Dworkin's *Taking Rights Seriously*
James G. March's *Exploration and Exploitation in Organisational Learning*
Ikujiro Nonaka's *A Dynamic Theory of Organizational Knowledge Creation*
Griselda Pollock's *Vision and Difference*
Amartya Sen's *Inequality Re-Examined*
Susan Sontag's *On Photography*
Yasser Tabbaa's *The Transformation of Islamic Art*
Ludwig von Mises's *Theory of Money and Credit*

Macat Disciplines

Access the greatest ideas and thinkers across entire disciplines, including

Postcolonial Studies

Roland Barthes's *Mythologies*
Frantz Fanon's *Black Skin, White Masks*
Homi K. Bhabha's *The Location of Culture*
Gustavo Gutiérrez's *A Theology of Liberation*
Edward Said's *Orientalism*
Gayatri Chakravorty Spivak's *Can the Subaltern Speak?*

Macat analyses are available from all good bookshops and libraries.

Access hundreds of analyses through one, multimedia tool.
Join free for one month **library.macat.com**

Macat Disciplines

Access the greatest ideas and thinkers across entire disciplines, including

AFRICANA STUDIES

Chinua Achebe's *An Image of Africa: Racism in Conrad's Heart of Darkness*

W. E. B. Du Bois's *The Souls of Black Folk*

Zora Neale Hurston's *Characteristics of Negro Expression*

Martin Luther King Jr.'s *Why We Can't Wait*

Toni Morrison's *Playing in the Dark: Whiteness in the American Literary Imagination*

Macat analyses are available from all good bookshops and libraries.

Access hundreds of analyses through one, multimedia tool.
Join free for one month **library.macat.com**

Macat Disciplines

Access the greatest ideas and thinkers across entire disciplines, including

FEMINISM, GENDER AND QUEER STUDIES

Simone De Beauvoir's
The Second Sex

Michel Foucault's
History of Sexuality

Betty Friedan's
The Feminine Mystique

Saba Mahmood's
*The Politics of Piety:
The Islamic Revival and
the Feminist Subject*

Joan Wallach Scott's
*Gender and the
Politics of History*

Mary Wollstonecraft's
*A Vindication of the
Rights of Woman*

Virginia Woolf's
A Room of One's Own

Judith Butler's
Gender Trouble

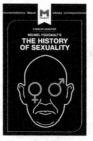

Macat analyses are available from all good bookshops and libraries.

Access hundreds of analyses through one, multimedia tool.
Join free for one month **library.macat.com**

Macat Disciplines

Access the greatest ideas and thinkers across entire disciplines, including

CRIMINOLOGY

Michelle Alexander's
The New Jim Crow: Mass Incarceration in the Age of Colorblindness

Michael R. Gottfredson & Travis Hirschi's
A General Theory of Crime

Elizabeth Loftus's
Eyewitness Testimony

Richard Herrnstein & Charles A. Murray's
The Bell Curve: Intelligence and Class Structure in American Life

Jay Macleod's
Ain't No Makin' It: Aspirations and Attainment in a Low-Income Neighborhood

Philip Zimbardo's
The Lucifer Effect

Printed in the United States
by Baker & Taylor Publisher Services